Don't Panic

The Psychology of Emergency Egress and Ingress

Jerome M. Chertkoff
and Russell H. Kushigian

PRAEGER

Westport, Connecticut
London

Library of Congress Cataloging-in-Publication Data

Chertkoff, Jerome M., 1936–
    Don't panic : the psychology of emergency egress and ingress /
Jerome M. Chertkoff and Russell H. Kushigian.
        p.   cm.
    Includes bibliographical references and index.
    ISBN 0–275–96268–7 (alk. paper)
        1. Buildings—Evacuation—Case studies.   2. Disasters—
Psychological aspects.   3. Fire—Psychological aspects.
4. Collective behavior.   5. Panic.   I. Kushigian, Russell H.
II. Title.
TH9410.C49   1999
628.9′2—dc21   98–47812

British Library Cataloguing in Publication Data is available.

Library of Congress Catalog Card Number: 98–47812
ISBN: 0–275–96268–7

First published in 1999

Praeger Publishers, 88 Post Road West, Westport, CT 06881
An imprint of Greenwood Publishing Group, Inc.
www.praeger.com

Printed in the United States of America

The paper used in this book complies with the
Permanent Paper Standard issued by the National
Information Standards Organization (Z39.48–1984).

10 9 8 7 6 5 4 3 2 1

Every reasonable effort has been made to trace the owners of copyright materials in this book, but
in some instances this has proven impossible. The author and publisher will be glad to receive information leading to more complete acknowledgments in subsequent printings of the book and in the
meantime extend their apologies for any omissions.

Books are to be returned on or before
the last date below.

7–DAY
LOAN

1 8 APR 2005

1 5 MAY 2006

– 4 MAY 2005

LIBREX –

"If you can keep your head when all about you
Are losing theirs and blaming it on you."
From *If* by Rudyard Kipling

"The most stringent protection of free speech would not protect a man in falsely
shouting 'fire' in a theater and causing a panic."
From the U.S. Supreme Court decision by Oliver Wendell Holmes in *Schneck v.
United States*

"Order and disorder are a matter of organization,
courage and cowardice are a matter of momentum."
From *The Art of War* by Sun Tzu

Contents

Illustrations

Preface

In writing this book, we had several goals in mind. It might benefit the reader to know these goals before proceeding.

One goal was to describe in a single book what actually happened in some of the most widely cited cases of disastrous emergency egress and ingress. Since the alleged events in these cases have been used to buttress various theoretical positions, it is important to know what really occurred.

A second goal, and the major one, was to compare cases of good versus bad emergency escape in order to determine the differences between rapid, efficient escape and slow, inefficient escape. We decided to restrict the number of bad cases to five, because adding further cases would not have altered our conclusions. Although additional negative cases consistent with our conclusions might have made those conclusions seem more convincing to some readers, the additional cases might have seemed like guilding the lily to other readers. We likewise decided to limit the number of good cases to two; because the evacuation of the World Trade Center involved the emergency evacuation of three separate buildings, the number of structures evacuated well was actually four. It was much harder to find good cases than bad, because good cases usually do not receive headlines and usually are not the subject of investigative reports.

A third goal was to use our conclusions to derive practical recommendations for achieving good emergency egress and ingress. Hence, the book ends with a chapter on prescriptions for success.

Our fourth goal was to write a book that is informative and interesting to both non-academics and academics.

We hope that we have achieved all of these goals.

Acknowledgments

We want to thank our wives, Sharon and Elise, our children, Nicolay, Darren, Alina, and Melissa, Russell's parents, Rose and Jack, brother, Marvin, sister-in-law, Janet, sister, Julia, brother-in-law, Charlie, nephews, Matthew and John, son-in-law, Matthew, and everyone else who listened to our tales of emergency escape with avid interest, some of whom even said they would buy a book on the subject.

We want to express our great appreciation to the two secretaries of the Psychology Department of Indiana University who put forth so much effort on the book, Sheryl Mobley and Karen Jukes Craig.

Chapter 1

Introduction

On Friday, December 27, 1895, the United Oriental and Dramatic Company of Boston was to perform the opera *Alexander*, in Yiddish, at the Front Street Theatre in Baltimore, Maryland. A capacity crowd of about 2,700 people had come to see *Alexander*. Most of the audience were Jewish immigrants, mainly from Poland and Russia, and their families.

The Front Street Theatre was a large, old building. The main entrances, four in number, were on Front Street. Each entrance had two sliding doors. Inside the lobby, to the left and right, were two staircases ascending to the first and second galleries. The stairways to the first gallery were about 10 to 12 feet wide, and the stairways to the second gallery were about 5 to 6 feet wide. Each staircase had one sharp turn. The inner doors to the auditorium were swinging doors that opened both ways.

The theater was lighted by gas, and there had been recent problems with leaking gas. When the opera *Alexander* was performed there on Christmas night, the first of two performances, some people became ill from inhaling gas, one person even lost consciousness. During a rehearsal on December 26, the smell of gas was again quite pronounced. The problem was brought to the attention of A. S. Miles, a director and treasurer of the company owning the theater. He had his nephew, William Miles, handle the problem. Although the nephew allegedly had some knowledge of pipe fitting, he was not a plumber. William worked on the gas pipes, mending some leaks and installing some new brackets.

On the night of December 27, 1895, the smell of gas was apparent to many in the theater long before the 8:00 P.M. curtain time. Employees tried to find the source of the leak, but without immediate success. They continued to look.

At 8:00 P.M., the lights were dimmed, and the orchestra began the overture. As the overture was coming to an end, a stagehand named Wil, carrying a lighted candle in order to see in the dimmed theater, was searching for the leak in the first gallery. When the candle came close to the source of the gas leak, either a cracked pipe or a loose connection, a highly visible jet of flame appeared. The flame, fed by the gas, continued to burn. A number of people cried, "Fire!"

When the overture was completed, stage carpenter Matthew Cavanaugh received the signal to raise the curtain. As he was doing so, he heard a commotion in the audience. According to Cavanaugh:

At first I thought it was caused by a fight, but when the curtain got half way up I saw the little flame in the gallery. It was not more than a foot long and couldn't have done any harm, as it was against a brick wall. Young Miles and I ran to the cellar and turned off the meter leading to the leak. This put out the flame. There was no cause for alarm, but the cry of fire seemed to come from all parts of the house. (Those leaking pipes, 1895, p. 10)

Matthew Cavanaugh and William Miles, the person who had tried to fix the leaks previously, turned off the gas to the main part of the house. Suddenly, there was darkness. The darkness was not quite total, however, because lights on the wall in the upper part of the house were controlled by a different meter. Miles then turned off the gas to the footlights and the circle. The meter that controlled the gas to the lights in the front of the building and the corridors was in a different part of the cellar. Someone else turned off that meter.

Many rushed for the exits. Those who originally hesitated soon joined the surging crowd. The actors on stage shouted to the crowd in Yiddish and in English that there was no danger, but few paid attention to them.

The one special policeman in the building, Simon Otto, was standing in the orchestra section at the rear of the middle aisle when the exiting began. There were ushers in the orchestra section, where there was reserved seating, but there were no ushers in the galleries, where seating was by general admission. Otto and the ushers tried to calm the people and regulate the flow, but with limited success. Otto went out to the gallery stairs and tried to control the crowd there.

Otto described the situation: "I saw several persons trampled under foot. Their bodies came sliding down the steps under the trampling of hundreds of other persons. Several persons jumped over the railing at the steps and escaped in that way. I was knocked down, but managed to get upon my feet again unharmed" (Theatre employees, 1895, p. 8).

The stairs were especially dangerous. They were narrow, and the steps increased the risk of a fall. If someone fell, the surge of people from behind would make it difficult to avoid stepping on or tripping over the person on the ground.

The gas was turned on again, but the return of light did little to calm the people. People pushed their way forward, trying to escape the nonexistent fire. Jams occurred at the front entrances, halting the egress into Front Street.

The full horror of what people experienced during the rush to exit is reflected in the following descriptions by survivors:

Then the people all made a rush for the doors. I became frightened and started to get up, but was knocked down, trampled on and pushed about the floor like a bunch of rags. My skirt was torn off, my cape lost, and I was nearly suffocated by persons walking on me. (Went back for his wife, 1895, p. 8)

When I reached the stairway the pressure on me was terrible. Women were screaming, children crying and men pushing in a wild effort to get out. It was horrible. Nobody knew what had happened. I felt the crowd pushing and shoving me and then I fell, and remember nothing more until I recovered consciousness at the bottom of the stairs. (Told by young girls, 1895, p. 8)

Suddenly I heard some one yell "fire," and I grasped little Sarah by the hand and told her to sit still, but when I saw every one trying to get to the door, I also tried. Just as we got to the door we were thrown down and the crowd trampled on us both.

I began to feel dizzy when someone grabbed me by the hair and pulled me out on the pavement. I cried out for Sarah, but I got no answer and thought that perhaps she, too, might have escaped. [Unfortunately Sarah Seigle, 10 years old, did not escape alive.] (Sarah Seigle's death, 1895, p. 8)

When I reached the entrance I was horrified at the sight there. People were packed into the opening. Many appeared to be on their heads, while others were piled up. The firemen and patrolmen were working nobly, and it was not long before a passage was effected. Besides a few bruises, I am all right. (Various experiences, 1895, p. 8)

Someone had called the fire department, and firefighters and police soon arrived. The police cleared the jams at the front entrance, allowing a flow of people out onto Front Street.

Often relatives or friends were separated in the rush to exit. Outside, they sought one another. Some parents, unable to locate their children, attempted to reenter. The police and firefighters tried to restrain them.

The crowd outside massed around the front exits, and the police were unable to establish control. The police ordered a fire engine hose turned on the crowd. The force of the water dispersed the people, driving them away from the front of the theater.

The police entered the theater and faced the horror of 23 dead bodies. These people had been trampled to death, suffocated by the exiting crowd. The majority of those killed, 14 of the 23, were children, 14 years of age and under. Perhaps as many as 100 others were seriously injured.

A jury of inquest was convened. They reached the conclusion that the cry of fire was "without foundation" and that there was no "just ground" for the "stampede," because the gas leakage was minimal and could have remained burning for hours without danger. If the audience had remained seated, no one would have been injured, but instead the audience became panic stricken. Blame rested entirely on the audience.

Why did the audience become panic stricken? *The Baltimore Sun* offered one possible explanation: "The audience was composed almost altogether of Russian and Polish Jews. They are naturally of a very nervous and excitable temperament" (Out went the gas, 1895, p. 8).

How can one explain the behavior of people in the Front Street Theatre that night? Was the rush to exit that resulted in the trampling to death of 23 people, mainly children, due to irrational panic or was it due to some rational decision-making process aimed at self-survival? In this book we will strive to understand why people behaved as they did in a situation such as the one at the Front Street Theatre.

Exiting as part of a group from an enclosed space, or entering for that matter, is something most of us do often. People enter or leave a bus, a subway car, a train, or a plane in conjunction with others. People enter or leave rooms, enter or leave buildings in combination with others. Usually the consequence of poor pedestrian traffic flow is a loss of time, which can be frustrating and costly. On rare occasions, the exiting involves an emergency situation, where the consequences of delay are extremely negative. In the extreme, failure to exit quickly can mean severe injury or death.

In this book, we will be concerned with the coordination of traffic flow in groups of pedestrians. We will examine that flow in both entering and exiting enclosed spaces. What factors affect the traffic flow of pedestrians? When is it orderly and efficient and when is it disorderly, in the extreme resulting in the blocking of doorways and people being crushed to death?

The remaining chapters are organized in the following manner. In chapter 2, we will cover the major theories of pedestrian traffic flow in an emergency. In chapters 3–7, we will examine five interesting historical cases of the failure to achieve smooth traffic flow. For counterpoint, in chapters 8 and 9 we will look at two cases of extremely successful traffic flow. In chapter 10, we will attempt to draw some conclusions and relate those conclusions back to the theories presented in chapter 2 and the examples of unsuccessful and successful traffic flow given in chapters 3–9. In chapter 11, we will give prescriptions for success in facilitating efficient traffic flow.

A word is in order about how we picked the seven cases. Each of the seven case histories was selected because it fit most or all of the following five criteria. One, it was cited frequently in the research literature. Two, it was at an extreme end of the continuum from very bad to very good pedestrian traffic flow. Three, for the failures, it involved a large number of deaths. Four, there was a large amount of reliable information about the event, preferably including books and published investigative reports, not just newspaper and magazine accounts. Five, each case represented a different type of environmental situation.

The Iroquois Theatre Fire and the Cocoanut Grove Night Club Fire are perhaps the two most cited cases of extremely poor emergency evacuation in literature. Both involved horrendous loss of life. Both were the subjects of books and investigative reports.

The Hartford Circus Fire is rarely cited in the literature on emergency evacuation, but it should be. The evacuation had severe problems. The loss of life was high, though significantly less than at the Iroquois or Cocoanut Grove fires. The Hartford Circus Fire has been analyzed in an investigative report and a book. Furthermore, it represents an interesting variation on the typical case of evacuation from a fixed structure, involving instead evacuation from a circus tent.

The Beverly Hills Supper Club Fire, although a second case of a night club fire, met all the other criteria. It is widely cited in research papers and books on collective behavior. The evacuation, at times, seemed to be extremely dysfunctional. The death toll was high, equivalent to that at the Hartford Circus Fire. There is a large amount of information available about the event, including multiple investigative reports, a book, and a questionnaire research analysis.

The Who Concert Stampede is a widely cited case of horribly dysfunctional pedestrian traffic flow. The number who died was not large, but the fact that anyone could die under such circumstances seems astounding. The Who Concert Stampede represented a very different kind of situation than the other four, because the disaster occurred as people entered a structure rather than when leaving it.

The two cases of good pedestrian traffic flow were taken from recent case histories. The evacuation of a Trans World Airlines jet was an impressive example of efficient pedestrian traffic flow. There was an investigative report of the incident. Furthermore, it represented a different environmental situation than the other cases, being a case of evacuation from an airplane.

The evacuation of the World Trade Center following a bomb explosion appeared to be amazingly well handled. Although a recent event, information beyond just the newspaper accounts is available. It represents a case of evacuation from high-rise office buildings and from a hotel, unlike any of the other cases.

In conclusion, we were looking for prominent extreme cases about which there is a lot of reliable information, while trying, at the same time, to include a variety of different environmental circumstances. We did not pick our examples because they fit some theoretical bias. In fact, in almost all of the cases, we knew very little about them when we began our research. In a number of cases, what we discovered to be true came as a surprise, being contrary to the descriptions in certain articles and books on dysfunctional pedestrian traffic flow.

Chapter 2

Theories of Emergency Egress and Ingress

In order to explain why people behaved as they did at the Front Street Theatre, we need a theory of pedestrian traffic flow in an emergency. A theory is a set of assumptions that interprets some phenomenon. A good theory not only explains the occurrence of a particular phenomenon, but also if it does not always happen, the probability that it will. In this chapter, we will examine the most prominent theories about emergency egress and ingress.

PANIC THEORIES

All of the theories that we classify as panic theories view panic as a likely result when a crowd tries to exit under conditions of high threat. Panic is usually defined as involving two elements, high emotional excitement and irrational, nonadaptive flight. The theories in this section offer explanations for the occurrence of panic, and since panic does not always ensue, they explain what factors make the occurrence of panic more or less likely.

Le Bon

Initial attempts to explain the behavior of people exiting or entering a structure under time pressure because of some real or perceived danger can be found in early theories of crowd psychology. The most widely cited theory is that of Gustave Le Bon, as propounded in his 1895 book *The Crowd*.

For Le Bon, a crowd is not just any gathering of people. A "psychological crowd," to use his term, exists only when the sentiments and ideas of the people all take the same direction. When a psychological crowd occurs, the usual conscious personalities of the people are replaced by their unconscious personalities. What did Le Bon mean by the term "unconscious personality"? The unconscious personality is composed of the common characteristics of all members of a race as passed on via heredity.

The predominance of the unconscious personality in a psychological crowd is due to three causes: (1) large numbers of people possessing feelings of invincibility due to numerical strength and hiding behind a cloak of anonymity; (2) contagion of sentiments and acts; (3) heightened suggestibility. These causes make people feel, think, and act similarly and in a way they would not do individually.

The result of the dominance of the unconscious personality is that people in crowds act irrationally—impulsively, without reason, in the absence of judgment and critical evaluation—and emotionally—exhibiting irritability and the exaggeration of sentiments. In a crowd, intellectual functioning sinks to the lowest common denominator existing in all members of a race by inheritance, and emotionality is reduced to the most basic instinctive displays of emotion. People in a crowd exhibit those characteristics "which are almost always observed in beings belonging to inferior forms of evolution—in women, savages, and children, for instance" (Le Bon, 1960, p. 36).

Le Bon was certainly racist and sexist, and he did not think highly of children—not an attractive person to most of us today. However, his assertion that people in crowds are highly emotional and irrational had a lasting impact.

Le Bon's theory contains certain qualifications. A gathering of people might not form a psychological unity, a psychological crowd, and if they did not, the assumptions about a psychological crowd would not hold. Furthermore, the actions of crowds are susceptible to influence by leaders, since Le Bon assumed that people in a psychological crowd instinctively place themselves under the authority of a leader. The domination of an individual over a crowd comes through prestige, either acquired, such as via money or position, or personal, through one's own charisma. A leader influences the beliefs of a crowd in three ways: (1) affirmation, meaning assertions free of reasoning and proof; (2) repetition; and (3) contagion—once some are influenced by repeated affirmations, their feelings, beliefs, and acts will spread to others.

McDougall

William McDougall, while a professor of psychology at Harvard, presented a somewhat similar theoretical analysis in his 1920 book *The Group Mind*. McDougall believed that the prime movers of social behavior are certain basic instincts, one of which is the flight-fear instinct. According to McDougall, an instinct is an inherited tendency that causes a person to attend to objects of a certain class, to experience a specific kind of emotional excitement upon perceiving such an object, and to act toward it in a particular manner. The flight instinct is always accompanied by the emotional excitement of fear, and a variety of objects can release it. One object class that releases the flight-fear instinct is the occurrence of fear and flight in others. While the fear and flight of others causes us to feel fear and have an impulse to flee, if a few others are fearless, or appear so, the release of the flight-fear instinct may be checked. "If the danger is not too imminent and obvious, the panic may die away, leaving men ashamed and astonished at the intensity of their emotion and the violent irrational character of their behavior" (McDougall, 1920, p. 37).

La Piere

Richard La Piere, a Stanford sociologist, dealt with panic behavior in his 1938 book *Collective Behavior*. When a stimulus is defined by people as a source of danger, panic behavior may occur. "Thus, the definition of smoke in a theater as a source of danger may turn a passive audience into a shrieking, milling mass which clogs the aisles and jams the exits" (La Piere, 1938, p. 437).

During a crisis such as a fire, regimental behavior, such as filing out in a specific order, might occur. Training groups in patterns of responding and/or obeying direction by leaders can produce regimental behavior. Regimental behavior is coordinated and predictable. Panic behavior is its antithesis, uncoordinated interaction with unpredictable consequences, making it in La Piere's view "always inadequate in terms of the majority of the group" (La Piere, 1938, p. 437).

For La Piere, then, panic behavior is caused by two factors: (1) the occurrence of a crisis, an event defined by those in the situation as a source of danger, and (2) the lack of regimentation and/or the lack of regimental leadership.

One could cite other theoreticians with essentially identical ideas, including Sigmund Freud in his 1922 book *Group Psychology and the Analysis of the Ego*, but these will suffice. All believed that in a situation of perceived danger, people in crowds are quite likely to be highly emotional and engage in uncoordinated flight, leading to trampling of others and jams. Training in coordinated behavior or fearless, resolute leadership are ways to combat the likelihood of panic. This line of theorizing reached its pinnacle in the theory of collective behavior by sociologist Neal Smelser.

Smelser

The most detailed of all panic theories is Smelser's Value-Added Theory, first presented in his 1963 book *Theory of Collective Behavior*. Smelser's theory is a general theory of collective action, applicable to crazes, hostile outbursts, and social movements as well as panic. We shall consider only panic. Smelser defined panic as collective flight based on a hysterical belief, the belief that an ambiguous element in the environment represents a severe danger.

A series of factors, in sequence, adds an element, a value, that moves the collectivity toward panic. Each factor is necessary, but not sufficient, to cause panic. The factors are, in sequence: (1) structural conduciveness; (2) structural strain; (3) growth and spread of a generalized hysterical belief; (4) precipitating factor; (5) mobilization of participants for action; and (6) absence of operation of social control.

1. *Structural conduciveness*. The structure of the environment is such that entrapment is possible, even likely. An inadequate number of exits, locked exits, or narrow passageways are examples of elements of structural conduciveness. If the structural elements allow easy escape, then panic will not occur.

2. *Structural strain*. Strain refers to any factor that impairs adequate functioning. Stress of any sort creates a strain. Fire in a building creates strain. Situations create a strain on people when there is ambiguity as to how to achieve a specific goal, such as how to escape from a burning building. Conflict among people for limited resources, such as access to exits, creates strain. These are only examples of possible sources of strain, for Smelser does not give an exhaustive typology of all

forms of strain.

3. *Growth and spread of a generalized hysterical belief.* Given certain ambiguity about the situation confronting people, they must interpret it, give it meaning. That interpretation constitutes the generalized belief that identifies and evaluates the source of the strain and specifies appropriate responses to the strain. A hysterical belief is a belief that an ambiguous aspect of the environment has the power to threaten or destroy. The sequence of factors leading to the development of a hysterical belief are as follows: There is an ambiguous situation that gives rise to anxiety, and the anxiety leads to a redefinition of the situation as one certain to harm or destroy, resulting in deep pessimism or terrible fear.

4. *Precipitating factor.* Some specific event precipitates the panic. For example, a shout of "Fire!" could precipitate panic.

5. *Mobilization of participants for action.* Some person or people initiate the mobilization to action. For example, someone mobilizes the participants to panic by rushing for the exit.

6. *Absence of operation of social control.* Norms can specify behavior in certain circumstances, thereby reducing anxiety, fear, and social disorganization. Fire drills can provide such norms. Norms, such as "save your loved ones," can provide general directives for action, thereby reducing the occurrence of panic. People acting out a leadership role, such as a teacher directing children to safety, can control panic. If norms and controls are absent or inadequate, panic occurs.

To repeat, all factors in the sequence are necessary because each adds essential value. Although each factor in the sequence is necessary, a given stimulus can act as both a later factor and an earlier factor. For example, the cry of "Fire!" when no fire is observable can cause strain, give rise to a hysterical belief, and be a precipitating event.

DECISION-MAKING THEORIES

Decision-making theories assume that human behavior, whether there is danger or not, results from an attempt by the people involved to make decisions calculated to obtain good outcomes for themselves. Decisions may lead to actions that turn out badly, but if so, that is because of incomplete or faulty information, errors in evaluating the information, or a poor decision-making process. All of these theories present an analysis of people's evaluation of the situation—the informational basis for the decision process—and how they use that evaluation to make their decisions.

Mintz

In a 1951 paper entitled "Non-adaptive Group Behavior," social psychologist Alexander Mintz challenged the view that the behavior of people in crowds was irrational. Mintz maintained that behavior such as knocking others down and trampling over them resulted from the reward structure of the situation. In a situation such as a theater fire, cooperation with others so that all wait their turn is likely to be beneficial to the group, because the greatest number exit safely, and beneficial to the individual, because the individual's likelihood of exiting is maximized. "Thus at a theater fire, if everyone leaves in an orderly manner, everybody is safe, and an individual waiting for his turn is not sacrificing his interests" (Mintz, 1951, p. 151).

The reward structure changes, however, when even a few others push. If others are pushing, then an individual will feel that his/her chances of exiting safely are threatened. Allowing others to push ahead uncontested may maximize the number of the group exiting safely, but your own chances of escape are reduced as others push past you. So you push also, in an effort to maximize your likelihood of exiting safely.

Mintz did not deny that danger increases emotionality and that the heightened emotionality of some might increase the emotionality of others, but he argued that there was no direct causal relationship between heightened emotionality and non-adaptive behavior.

In summary, Mintz maintained that cooperation is rewarding to the individual provided that all others cooperate, but that competitive actions benefit the individual if others are behaving competitively.

Thus at a theater fire it pays not to push if everybody cooperates, but if a few uncooperative individuals block the exits by pushing, then any individual who does not push can expect that he will be burned. Pushing becomes the advantageous (or least disadvantageous) form of behavior for individuals, and disorder leading to disastrous consequences spreads rapidly. (Mintz, 1951, p. 151)

People were not reverting to innate basic instinctual tendencies. They were not driven by uncontrolled fear. They were behaving rationally, in a way that maximized their own chances of exiting. If others cooperated, then one's own chances of escaping were maximized by cooperating also, but if others competed, then one's own chances of escaping were maximized by competing also.

Kelley, Condry, Dahlke, and Hill, in a 1965 paper entitled "Collective Behavior in a Simulated Panic Situation," critiqued the Mintz analysis, noting that it did not explain the onset of competitive behavior. If cooperation maximized the individual's likelihood of escape, given that others were cooperating, why would anyone be the first to push or? Pushing and shoving when others were not would reduce that person's chances of escape according to Mintz, because one's chances of es-cape are supposedly maximized by cooperating when all others are cooperating.

That is certainly an important point. Either Mintz was wrong when he asserted that cooperation maximizes the likelihood of escape if all others are cooperating or he needed to add an additional factor to explain the onset of competition.

Brown

Roger Brown, in his 1965 book *Social Psychology*, proposed that the situation confronting people in groups when trying to escape is analogous to a famous type of decision-making conundrum called the prisoner's dilemma. The prisoner's dilemma is a type of social interaction matrix, one that contains a specific pattern of outcomes.

The name "prisoner's dilemma" comes from the following real world example of this type of matrix, attributed to mathematician A. W. Tucker by R. Duncan Luce and Howard Raiffa in their 1957 book, *Games and Decisions*:

Two suspects are taken into custody and separated. The district attorney is certain that they are guilty of a specific crime, but he does not have adequate evidence to convict them at a trial. He points out to each prisoner that each has two alternatives: to confess to the crime the police are sure they have done, or not to confess. If they both do not confess, then the district attorney states he will book them on some very minor trumped-up charge such as petty larceny and illegal possession of a weapon, and they will both receive minor punishment; if they both confess they will be prosecuted, but he will recommend less than the most severe sentence; but if one confesses and the other does not, then the confessor will receive lenient treatment for turning state's evidence whereas the latter will get "the book" slapped at him. (Luce & Raiffa, 1957, p. 95)

The dilemma of the two prisoners can be represented as a two-person social interaction matrix (see Table 1). In a two-person matrix the alternatives of one person or "player" are listed in rows, hence that player is called the row player, and the alternatives of the other person are listed in columns, hence that player is called the column player. Since both prisoners have the same two choices, not confess or confess, these choices are listed in two separate rows for the row player, Prisoner A, and in two separate columns for the column player, Prisoner B. The intersections of row choices and column choices are called cells. Since there are two row choices and two column choices, there are two times two, or four, cells: both do not confess; A does not confess and B confesses; A confesses and B does not confess; both confess. In each cell the outcomes or payoffs of that cell for both the row player and the column player are presented.

Table 1
Payoff Matrix for Prisoners A and B in a Prisoner's Dilemma

		B	
		Not confess (Cooperation)	Confess (Competition)
A	Not confess (Cooperation)	-2 for A; -2 for B	-10 for A; 0 for B
	Confess (Competition)	0 for A; -10 for B	-5 for A; -5 for B

Tucker, in his scenario, did not give exact outcomes for the cells in the matrix, so we will make up prison sentences that seem to fit. The prisoner's dilemma might be represented by the payoff matrix in Table 1. If both do not confess, they both receive minor punishment for lesser crimes—two years in prison, or -2 for each since years in prison are negative. If they both confess, they will be prosecuted for the more severe crime, but they will receive less than the maximum sentence—five years in prison, or -5 for each. If one confesses and one does not confess, the confessor receives lenient treatment—a suspended sentence and no years in prison—and the one who does not confess will get the maximum sentence—10 years in prison, or -10.

If you were Prisoner A, how would you analyze the situation? You might say to yourself, "If B does not confess, I receive -2 if I do not confess and 0 if I confess. It is better to spend no years in prison than two years in prison, so if I could be sure that B will not confess, I should confess. But suppose B confesses. Then I receive -10 if I do not confess and -5 if I confess. It is better to spend five years in prison than 10 years in prison, so if I could be sure that B will confess, I should confess. My choice is clear. Regardless of B's choice, I do better by confessing. It is logical for me to confess."

Is it really logical to confess? Prisoner A and Prisoner B have the same choices with the same outcomes, so the logic applying to one also applies to the other. Prisoner B does better by confessing regardless of A's choice (0 is better than -2 and -5 is better than -10). So if both reason in this way, both will confess. Both will then get five years in prison, the outcomes in the confess-confess cell. Now the interesting thing is that both would be better off if they both made the opposite choice. The outcomes for both are only two years in prison if they both do not confess and five years if they do. Perhaps then the logical thing to do is to not confess.

The prisoner's dilemma is a symmetrical matrix, in that the decision-making dilemma confronting each of the two people is identical. Each has two choices, one is cooperation (do not confess), and the other is competition (confess). Regardless of the choice made by the other, each prisoner's outcome is maximized by making the competitive choice. Although for both, the competitive choice maximizes one's own outcomes regardless of the choice of the other, both are worse off, not better, in the mutual competition cell than the mutual cooperation cell. Therein lies the dilemma.

If the prisoner's dilemma is analogous to escape from a burning building, then competitive behavior should maximize one's probability of escaping regardless of whether others are cooperating or competing, but if all compete the probability of escape is lower than if all cooperate. According to Roger Brown, that is exactly the case when trying to escape an entrapment situation.

Brown presented the matrix for entrapment shown in Table 2. The outcomes are ordered from most favorable to least favorable: ++, +, -, --. If the others in the group take turns and do not push, you have a reasonably good chance of getting out alive by doing the same (+), but if you push ahead to the exit, you will have a still higher likelihood of escape (++). In the latter case you go right through to the front and out. If on the other hand, the others in the group rush the exit, you will have little chance of escaping by waiting your turn (--) and a somewhat better chance of escaping if you fight the others for access to the exit (-). So rushing pell mell to the exit maximizes your chances of escaping regardless of what the others in the group do. Yet all waiting their turns is better for all than all rushing for the exit.

Brown realized that his analysis of escape as a straightforward two-person prisoner's dilemma was somewhat simplistic for two reasons. First, probably not everyone in the situation has the same matrix. People further from the exit probably have different matrix values than people closer to the exit. Second, in the standard prisoner's dilemma, each side has the same number of people, while in his analysis, the person on one side is only one and the group on the other side is composed of many people. It seems likely that the actions of one person will have less effect on the group than the actions of all others in the group will have on one person. Nevertheless, Brown asserted that each person was confronted with a decision-making situation analogous to the situation of the prisoner's dilemma.

Table 2
Payoff Matrix for a Person (P) and a Group (G) in an Entrapment Situation

		G	
		Take turns	Rush exit
P	Take turns	+ for P; + for G	-- for P; ++ for G
	Rush exit	++ for P; -- for G	- for P; - for G

Brown maintained that since rushing for an exit maximized one's own chances of escaping, regardless of the actions of others in the group, rushing for an exit is the rational solution. For Brown, the interesting question was: Why didn't everyone rush for the exits immediately and always? Brown offered several explanations. First, if the fire is small enough so the threat to life is nonexistent, the matrix is no longer a prisoner's dilemma. If the fire is minor, the others' disapproval of pushing might be worse than inhaling a little smoke, so cooperation is better than competition if the others cooperate. Second, even in a severe fire, it may not be clear to people at the start that the situation is, in effect, like a prisoner's dilemma, and so based on past training in fire drills, everyone initially files out in turn. Only when the reality of the danger and the resulting payoff values become clear is there a rush to the exit.

It is possible, however, to argue that Brown was wrong in maintaining that the rational decision in a prisoner's dilemma is to compete. In a prisoner's dilemma situation, there are really two different logics, neither more rational than the other: compete, because that choice maximizes your outcomes regardless of the other's choice; cooperate, because mutual cooperation is better than mutual competition. Each way of reasoning is simply a different way of reaching a decision, given the same information. Initially, the decision-making process of most, but not all, may be dominated by the fact that mutual cooperation is better than mutual competition. Those who base their decision-making on the fact that competition maximizes their chance of escape regardless of the decisions of others to rush the exit. Once some push ahead, those who originally acted to achieve mutual cooperation realize that this is impossible, and they join the rush. If others compete, your outcome is better if you compete also.

An analysis of escape from entrapment as a type of prisoner's dilemma gives an answer to the question Mintz left unanswered: If cooperation is better than competition when others cooperate, how does the pushing and shoving begin? The answer is that cooperation does not maximize when others are cooperating. If others are filing out in turn, shoving ahead brings you immediately to the front and out. What stops everyone from doing that is the realization of many that all are best off with mutual cooperation rather than mutual competition. These people try to get their view across by urging others to file out in an orderly way. They may succeed, but they may not.

DISTRIBUTION OF URGENCY LEVELS THEORY

The only theory of this type is the one presented by Kelley, Condry, Dahlke, and Hill in their 1965 paper, "Collective Behavior in a Simulated Panic Situation." The main assumption of this theory is that the occurrence of blockages of exiting space depends upon the distribution of the levels of urgency to exit. One could apply this idea to a number of different kinds of distributions, but they focus on three main types: (1) the vast majority are situated at the low-urgency end of the scale with only a few spread out evenly across the higher levels; (2) there is a flat, level distribution with a small number at each level of urgency; or (3) the vast majority are at the high-urgency end of the scale with the remainder spread out evenly across the other levels.

Imagine a case where the vast majority of people have low urgency to exit. Such a situation might exist after a speech or concert or movie where the vast majority have no pressing engagements following the event. One or two might have to be somewhere else very soon, and they hurry out first. Several others may have a subsequent engagement but more time to get there, and they exit next. The vast majority, with no pressing need to leave, file out in a leisurely manner, free of competition for exit space and, therefore, free of jams. There might be some hesitations and false starts when a number arrive at the exit at the same time. An exchange of "After you."; "No, after you." might occur now and then; but overall there should be a steady flow, free of jams.

Imagine a case with a small number at each level of urgency. Such a situation might occur when different members of a small audience after one convention session must proceed to different convention sessions at varying distances away. The few people who have to attend the session farthest away at another hotel hurry out first. The next several people, who have to attend a session in a far-removed section of the same hotel, leave next. Those who have their next session at the end of the same hall leave next. Those who have their next session in the adjacent room leave last. As long as each group is small enough for the carrying capacity of the exit space, orderly exiting free of jams should occur.

A problem arises when the distribution of urgency levels contains a large number with a high urgency to leave. Those with high urgency rush to get out quickly, and a serious jam is likely as too many people try to exit at once. If after a large convention session, most people had only 15 minutes to get to the next session (which is 15 minutes away), there would be congestion and jams at the exits.

Jams are likely whenever factors cause a large number to have a high urgency to exit. One such factor would be the severity of the penalty for not exiting quickly. The greater the severity of the penalty for not exiting quickly, the greater the number of people with a high urgency to leave. Consequently, the greater the severity of the penalty is, the greater the likelihood of jams and entrapment is.

A second factor would be the time available to exit without penalty. The shorter the time available, the greater the number of people with a high urgency to exit. In other words, the shorter the time available is, the greater the likelihood of jams and entrapment is.

Yet another factor is the group size. The greater the number of people present, the more likely it is that a substantial number will have a high urgency to escape, just due to the sheer increase in numbers. Furthermore, large group size may have a psychological effect, causing those present to believe that due to the large crowd they will not exit in time unless they hurry. The larger the group present is, the greater the likelihood of jams and entrapment is.

These three factors do not constitute an exhaustive list. Any factor that leads to a large number of people in the crowd having a high urgency to leave will cause an increase in jams and greater entrapment.

Any factor that reduces the number of people having a high urgency to leave will cause a decrease in jams and less entrapment. One such factor is effective leadership. A demonstration of low urgency by a leader, especially when people are strongly inclined to follow that leader, should reduce the frequency of people with high urgency, thereby causing a more efficient exiting pattern.

We have presented the main theories of pedestrian traffic flow. How accurate and complete is each of these theories? In order to help us answer that question, we will examine in the succeeding chapters five cases of poor traffic flow and two cases of good traffic flow.

Point:
Case Histories of Failures

In the next five chapters, five dramatic case histories of poor pedestrian traffic flow are described in detail. Information about the events reported in these chapters and in the subsequent chapters on good pedestrian traffic flow was obtained from books, newspapers, magazines, journals, and investigative reports. (At the end of this book there is an annotated bibliography of these sources.) We tried to be as accurate as possible in describing what took place, but some caveats are in order.

Sometimes our sources contained statements of what people said, and we included such statements when we found them illuminating. Of course, people are unlikely to recall with perfect fidelity the exact words used by themselves or others, but we assumed that they did remember the gist of what was said.

Different people sometimes gave contradictory accounts of the same occurrences, and the same person sometimes gave different accounts over time. In such cases, we usually relied on the conclusions from investigative reports, which measured what people said against the physical evidence and which compared different accounts to determine which perceptions were held by the overwhelming majority. When what transpired still seemed to be in doubt, we tried to finesse the issue by presenting the facts that seemed to be uncontested, leaving the readers free to draw their own conclusions.

Newspaper accounts, especially first-day accounts, can be misleading, inaccurate, and incomplete. Undoubtedly, reporters tried hard to ascertain the facts, but initially there may be great uncertainty. Over time, a clearer, more certain, more comprehensive view tends to emerge. In general, when discrepancies existed across sources, we relied more heavily on later accounts, especially those from investigative reports and books.

We are dealing in these cases with history, and history is always subject to revision. New information may be discovered. Old information may be reinterpreted. We have tried to present the truth based on the present level of information. With history, it is always possible that our view of the truth will change.

Chapter 3

Iroquois Theatre Fire, December 30, 1903

Duane P. Schultz, in his often-cited 1964 book *Panic Behavior: Discussion and Readings*, stated that the huge death tolls at the Iroquois Theatre Fire and at the Cocoanut Grove Night Club Fire were due primarily to panic, not the fire. He concluded: "In both cases [Iroquois Theatre Fire and Cocoanut Grove Night Club Fire] the fire itself was brought quickly under control. It was the nonadaptive behavior which caused the majority of the deaths" (Schultz, 1964, p. 10).

We believe Schultz's view of these two events is not accurate. As you shall see in this and the following chapter, in both cases the fires were horrendous. The behavior of those trying to escape alive did affect the efficiency of the egress, but their behavior did not cause the majority of the deaths.

The Iroquois Theatre opened on November 23, 1903, in downtown Chicago. It was billed as the "most perfect theater in America" and as "absolutely fireproof." This attractive addition to the theater scene in Chicago had seats for over 1,700 people, the largest seating capacity of any theater in the city.

The main, south, entrance had five double-door openings, each 5 feet wide (see a on Figure 1). Beyond the entrance doors was a large vestibule. On the west end of the vestibule were the ticket offices, and on the east end, just inside the entrance doors, was a stairway leading to the theater office, over the vestibule on the balcony floor above.

Proceeding into the theater, you crossed the 18-foot vestibule and then passed through one of three door openings (see b on Figure 1). Each of these three openings was 7 feet wide, and each contained one single door wing and one double-folding door wing. You were now in the Grand Stair Hall (see Photograph 1). To your left and right were the start of two 8-foot-wide stairways leading to the floor above, the balcony floor. Across the open Grand Stair Hall were the entrances to the parquet floor (usually called the orchestra floor today). There were three door openings (see c on Figure 1) identical to the 7-foot-wide, single door–double folding door openings at the opposite end of the hall.

Figure 1
Iroquois Theatre Parquet (Main) Floor

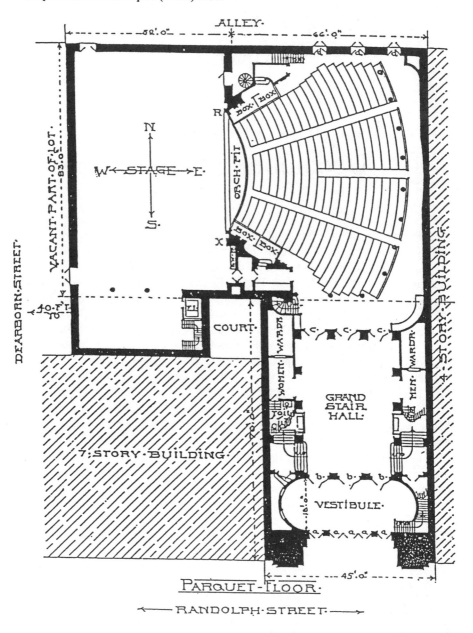

Theatre Historical Society of America. "*Retrospects* by Louis Guenzel. The IROQUOIS Theatre Fire."
Republished December 1993 by Theatre Historical Society of America, Elmhurst, IL.

Photograph 1. Iroquois Theatre Grand Stair Hall. The stairs were attractive, but they produced a deadly convergence of separate streams of people. Theatre Historical Society of America. *"Retrospects by Louis Guenzel. The IROQUOIS Theatre Fire."* Republished December 1993 by Theatre Historical Society of America, Elmhurst, IL.

The orientation of the inside of the theater was east and west. As you entered the parquet floor through the doors at the north end of the Grand Stair Hall, you were at the rear of the rows of seats facing left, or west, toward the stage.

An aisle, 12 feet wide, was between the entrance doors and the seats. The parquet floor had 19 curved rows of seats; each row was raised 5 inches above the row in front. The rows were divided by three 3-foot-wide aisles, with floors slanted to match the rise across the rows. The center aisle only ran from rows 9 through 19. At the north end of the parquet floor, across the interior of the theater from the entrance doors, was another aisle, 3 feet wide, that ran along the north wall. Off of this far aisle were three emergency exit doors, each with a succession of two pairs of double doors (see d on Figure 2). The aisle behind the last curved row of seats at the rear of the parquet floor varied in width and was just under 6 feet at its narrowest point.

On both sides at the front were two boxes. Above each pair of boxes was a third box, level with the front part of the balcony floor, the second floor. The higher boxes could be reached by narrow stairs behind the boxes on the parquet floor.

If you had a balcony or gallery seat, you did not cross the Grand Stair Hall. Instead you ascended stairs either to your left (west) or your right (east) immediately after entering the Grand Stair Hall from the vestibule. At the top of the stairs was a balcony promenade. In front of the top of the east wing of stairs was the rear entrance to the balcony floor (see e on Figure 2). You went up an additional three steps and entered through a 7-foot-wide door, fitted with a pair of double-folding doors. Those seemingly innocuous three steps up to the doorway would play a key role in the tragedy to come. A second entrance was located in the middle of the balcony. To reach the mid-balcony entrance, you had to walk down four steps on the balcony promenade. The mid-balcony entrance was 5 feet wide and had a double door (see f on Figure 2).

The balcony floor, or second floor, and the gallery floor, or third floor, were configured in the same way (see Figures 2 and 3). They both had 10 curved rows and five 3-foot-wide aisles, two outer aisles, and three interior aisles. Each row of the balcony was elevated about 14 inches, and the aisles had a step corresponding to each row. The gallery was tiered more steeply, about 27 inches of elevation for each row, and there were several steps in the aisle for each successive row. Both the balcony and gallery floors, like the parquet floor, had a passage behind the last row that was less than 6 feet wide at its narrowest point.

At the north end of both the balcony and gallery floors were three emergency exits. Each opening was 4 feet, 6 inches wide and had double glass doors on the inside and double steel doors on the outside. These doors opened onto 3-foot-wide fire escapes that ran down to the alley below.

To reach the gallery floor, the highest floor, you first ascended the east or west stairs to the balcony promenade. There were several ways to proceed from the balcony promenade. From the top of the west main stairs you could take a stairway straight ahead that led up to the front section of the gallery (see g on Figure 2). Alternatively, you could mount stairs on the north section of the balcony prome-

Figure 2
Iroquois Theatre Balcony Floor

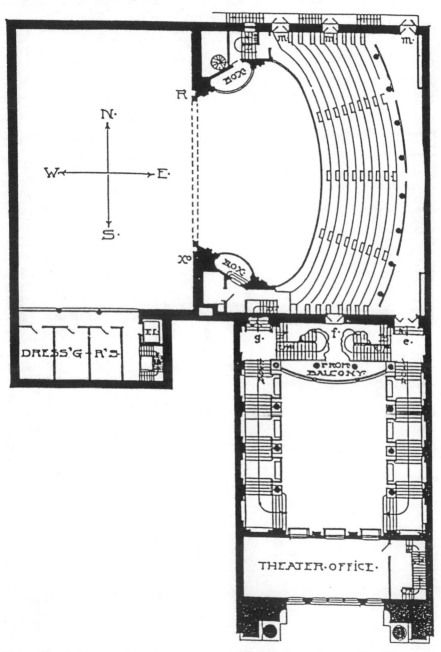

Theatre Historical Society of America. "*Retrospects* by Louis Guenzel. The IROQUOIS Theatre Fire."
Republished December 1993 by Theatre Historical Society of America, Elmhurst, IL.

Figure 3
Iroquois Theatre Gallery Floor

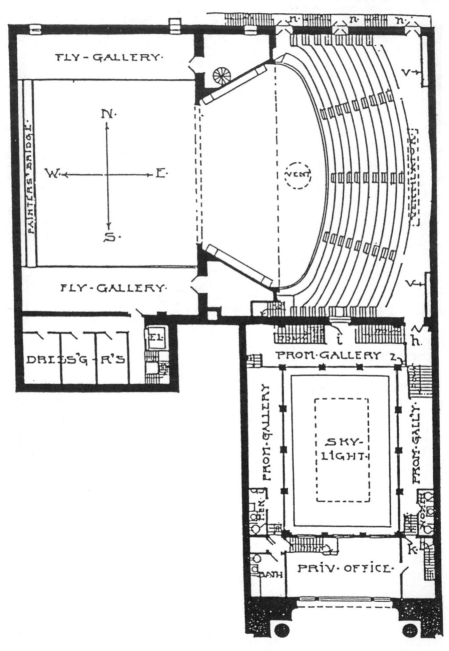

Theatre Historical Society of America. "*Retrospects* by Louis Guenzel. The IROQUOIS Theatre Fire." Republished December 1993 by Theatre Historical Society of America, Elmhurst, IL.

nade up to the gallery promenade. These stairs converged to a center platform about halfway up, then divided again into two flights, one heading north and one heading south, both ending at the gallery promenade.

The rear entrance to the gallery (see h on Figure 3), was 90 degrees to the left of the top of the stairs rising toward the east. The middle entrance to the gallery (see i on Figure 3) was reached by going around the stairwell of the stairs you had just ascended and then up an additional three steps. The mid-balcony opening had one double-bending door, and the rear balcony opening had one triple-bending door.

There were possible exits at the south ends of the east and west portions of the gallery promenade, though these exits would not normally be used by patrons attending a show. From the rear entrance to the gallery (see h on Figure 3), you could proceed straight ahead down a run of stairs, along the east section of the gallery promenade, and down a shorter run of stairs to a door (see k on Figure 3). If that door were open, you could turn left and then descend the stairway past the theater office on the balcony floor, down to the vestibule, and out the front entrance. From the south end of the west side of the gallery promenade, a short run of stairs took you to the entrance door of a private office on the gallery floor. If you could enter and exit that office, you could pass through it and thereby reach the same stairway accessed on the east side via the door marked k on Figure 3. That stairway, as stated before, led down to the vestibule beside the main entrance.

The stage was at the west end of the theater. At the southeast corner of the stage were steel double doors leading to seats on the parquet floor. Backstage there were two outside exit doors. One door was at the northwest corner of the stage, and it opened onto the alley behind the north wall of the theater. The other door was at the southwest corner of the stage, and it opened onto a vacant part of the lot, about 40 feet from Dearborn Street to the west.

The walls of the building were made of fireproof material. The stage curtains included a so-called fireproof curtain of asbestos. Most of the floors, walls, and stairs were made of tile, marble, plaster, and wrought iron, which could not burn.

The parquet, balcony, and gallery levels had wooden floors, and the aisles were covered with carpeting. There was a small amount of wooden molding on the walls of all three floors. Most of the interior doors were of wood, as were some handrails. The boxes had drapes. Other than that, the only flammable material in the seating section was in the seats themselves. The seats had cast iron frames with wooden arm supports. They were covered with a plush fabric and stuffed with a kind of hemp that, when burning, emitted a very dense, suffocating smoke. As events would show, it was an exaggeration to label the theater absolutely fireproof, but there were more safeguards and less flammable material than in most theaters of the time.

On Wednesday afternoon, December 30, 1903, the popular entertainer Eddie Foy was appearing in a matinee performance of *Mr. Blue Beard*, a musical extravaganza. The show had opened the new Iroquois Theatre on November 23, 1903. Since then it had been performed nightly with three matinees a week to large, enthusiastic crowds. The afternoon performance of December 30, at bargain matinee prices, had a capacity crowd plus several hundred standees.

Foy tried to get passes for his wife and children, but there were none available.

He brought his eldest son Bryan, then six, and seated him on a stool offstage to the right, a great vantage point.

Foy noted, as he took the stage during the first act, that there were a large number of mothers with their children, especially in the gallery. High school and college students, on vacation, were in abundance.

The first act went well. At the beginning of the second act, a double octet, eight men and eight women, were onstage for a song and dance number, "In the Pale of the Moonlight." The stage was lit to simulate moonlight, and all the auditorium lights were turned off.

Hanging suspended by ropes above the stage were 280 oil-painted backdrops, several of which were lowered for each set. Many of the drops contained delicate lace and sheer gauze. Some of the lights used to illuminate the set were dangerously close to these drops, and the wires to the lights were almost certainly overloaded. Earlier that year during a performance of the show in Cleveland, one of the lights had blown a fuse, setting a piece of drapery on fire. The fire had been extinguished quickly.

A floodlight set on a scaffold just outside the curtains (at X on Figure 1) ignited a bit of gauzy drapery. As in Cleveland, the fire was initially small. Stagehands tried to beat the fire out, but failed. Had there been adequate fire-fighting equipment at the Iroquois Theatre, the fire probably would have been extinguished quickly. There was one private firefighter backstage, but the sum total of fire-fighting equipment available to him was two tubes, 2.5 inches in diameter and 3 feet long, containing powder. Onstage were water standpipes with hose connections. However, the water supply system was not yet completed, so the pipes contained no water, and there were no hoses. Earlier that month, the district fire captain had complained to the Iroquois Theatre management and to his superiors that adequate fire-fighting equipment was inoperative or absent, but his warning had been ignored. The private firefighter and stagehands threw the powder on the flames, but the fire had become too large to control with the powder.

The fire spread to the other drops. A ticket taker at the main entrance, E. Leavitt, ran outside to a street alarm box and turned in the fire alarm.

On stage, the double octet continued with their song and dance routine. The auditorium lights were still out, as was required for that number.

The flames and the unsuccessful attempts to combat them were now visible to part of the audience. Someone yelled, "Fire!"

Eddie Foy was backstage in his costume as the character Sister Anne, preparing to go on. He hurried to the stool where his son Bryan was seated, picked up the boy and put him into the arms of a stagehand. Foy shouted to the stagehand, "Take my boy out!" (Foy & Harlow, 1928, p. 279). He watched them head for the rear exit doors at the back of the stage. Confident that his son would be safe, Foy then ran out on the stage through the faltering, but still performing, double octet.

The scenery above was ablaze. There was considerable dark smoke. Foy, dressed in a comical female costume, now stood before the audience. He noted that people in the balcony and gallery seemed especially frightened and on the verge of stampeding. He also noticed that the asbestos curtain had not been lowered yet.

To the audience, he shouted as loudly as he could, "Don't get excited. There's no danger. Take it easy" (Foy & Harlow, 1928, p. 280).

To the orchestra leader, he yelled, "Play! Start an overture—anything! But play!" (Foy & Harlow, 1928, p. 280). Most of the musicians fled, but a few remained and played.

To stagehands in the wings, he cried, "The asbestos curtain! For God's sake, doesn't anybody know how to lower this curtain?" (Foy & Harlow, 1928, p. 280). The asbestos curtain was lowered, but about two-thirds of the way down one end caught on a wire used to suspend a performer over the stage and the audience during a flying ballet number in the second act.

While Foy was onstage trying to quiet the crowd, most of the other members of the cast were exiting through the two backstage exterior doors. The opening of these doors created a strong draft that caused the asbestos curtain to flare out into the auditorium.

Above the stage in the ceiling were two great ventilators. Had they been open at that point in time, the draft would have sent the flames up in a column through those ventilators. Unfortunately, the counterweights needed to open the wings of these ventilators were missing, and the ventilators had temporarily been nailed closed when the theater opened. On December 30, 1903, five weeks later, the counterweights were still missing and the ventilators were still nailed shut. There were, however, open vents in the ceiling above the gallery and in the east wall behind the gallery (see Figure 4).

Suddenly, the fire seemed to explode, and a huge billow of flame rushed under the curtain toward the ceiling vents above the gallery. The flames brought immediate death to some, especially those in the gallery and the balcony. The audience was now in full flight to the exits.

After this ball of fire exploded into the theater, Eddie Foy, on the stage, felt blazing debris fall on him, setting his wig on fire. He looked up and saw the thin asbestos curtain disintegrate in flames. The last of the musicians had fled. Foy seemed to be the last person on stage.

Above him, the members of the flying ballet were up in the flies, about to begin. An elevator boy ran his car up through the flames into the flies and brought them down, but the lead performer, Nellie Reed, was burned so severely that she later died.

A number of performers were dressing in rooms under the stage. Some broke down locked outer doors in the basement to escape. Others escaped via a coal chute.

As Foy left the stage, the last ropes holding drops burned through and large amounts of burning material fell. All the theater lights—the house lights had never been turned on after being turned off for the moonlight scene—were now gone. Only the flames lit the inside of the building. Then another large ball of fire erupted into the interior, reaching all the way to the ceiling of the gallery.

People frequently found the exit paths blocked by locked doors. Of the five outside doors at the main entrance on Randolph Street (see a on Figure 1), two were locked and were broken open. Of the three doors at either end of the Grand Stair

Figure 4
Iroquois Theatre Section Following Main Axis of Auditorium

Theatre Historical Society of America. "*Retrospects* by Louis Guenzel. The IROQUOIS Theatre Fire."
Republished December 1993 by Theatre Historical Society of America, Elmhurst, IL.

Hall (see b and c on Figure 1), only one door was open at each end. Some, but not all, of the wings of doors there were broken open. All three emergency doors on the north side of the parquet floor (see d on Figure 1) were shut, and the middle one never was opened.

The people in the parquet fared best. The relatively few deaths or injuries to people on the ground floor resulted from flames, though they passed over most on the ground floor, people jumping on them from the balcony or gallery, or people knocking them down and trampling on them. According to Foy, for the most part, people on the parquet floor filed out in an orderly way. At the rear of the ground floor, a few were knocked down and stepped on, but ushers and police, who had arrived by then, rescued those who had been knocked to the floor.

In the balcony, the middle door (see f on Figure 2) was locked and attempts to force it open failed. The rear balcony doorway had one of its double wings open, but one wing remained closed (see e on Figure 2). Of the three emergency fire escape exits in the north wall of the balcony (see m on Figure 2), only the west one, closest to the stage, could be opened. So people in the balcony had only two ways out, the one open door to the fire escape and the one open wing to the rear door.

Afterward an usher admitted he could have opened the second wing of the rear balcony door, and he was at a loss to explain why he had not done so. Management had given orders that the ushers should leave the doors closed until the next to last act. Furthermore, ushers and other personnel had received no instructions about what to do in case of fire.

Those exiting the balcony at the rear had to go down three steps (see e on Figure 2) in darkness to a platform, then straight ahead down the east wing of the main stairs. These initial three steps down turned out to be disastrous. People tripped and fell on these steps. Others fell on top of them. People tried to scramble over the pile. In and behind the doorway, totally blocking the exit, was a pile of people, perhaps 6 feet high.

Those who had escaped successfully before the pile of people blocked the rear door of the balcony met a surge of people coming down the stairs from the gallery. The people descending from the gallery entered the stream from the rear door of the balcony at a right angle. In this bottleneck, some were knocked down and stepped on. Again, an interlocking pile of people formed, slowing escape down the main east stairway.

Those who exited the balcony onto the fire escape soon found their way down blocked by flames escaping through the exit doors below. Painters working in the Northwestern University Building across the way put out a ladder to the fire escape platform. One man tried to crawl over it, but the ladder slipped off the icy landing, and he fell to his death. The painters then bridged the gap with more stable wooden planks. Twelve people successfully escaped before fire erupted out of the door, killing those still on the platform.

The greatest loss of life was in the gallery, where the flames were drawn by the vents there. The exit at the front of the gallery (see g on Figure 2) was closed, but it was forced open and a few escaped through it before the fire inundated the gallery. The middle gallery exit (see i on Figure 3) was closed and eventually consumed by fire. The rear exit (see h on Figure 3) was open, and most people successfully exiting the gallery left by that door. However, in the dark many forgot to make an immediate right turn to descend the stairs to the balcony promenade. Instead they went straight, going down the stairs in front of them, along the east wing of the gallery promenade, and then down some more steps to a door (see k on Figure 3)—which was locked. They tried to retrace their steps, but by then fire had burst forth from the rear balcony doorway (see h on Figure 3), sealing off access to the stairway outside of that doorway. Some were killed by the fire. Others died after jumping over the balustrade to the floor below.

Firefighters and police responded quickly to the alarm. The flames, the dark smoke, and the absence of interior lights hampered their efforts to rescue people and put out the fire. Some firefighters and police entered through the main entrance and ascended the east stairs of the Grand Stair Hall. On the platform at the top of the east stairs and at the rear doorway to the balcony, they found two piles of bodies that blocked further egress from the balcony. People were twisted together and difficult to free. Some in the piles were still alive. The firefighters and police rescued the living and carried out the dead. Within the balcony and gallery sections, piles of dead were found next to closed exits and in the walkway behind the last row of seats. Some were burned to death or overcome by smoke in the aisles, while others were still in their seats facing forward, as they had been when the surge of fire ended their lives.

Some firefighters tried to cross the planks laid down by the painters in the Northwestern University Building. Initially they were beaten back by surges of fire, but some eventually gained access to the interior of the balcony in that way.

The police tried to cordon off Randolph Street from State Street on one side to Dearborn Street on the other; however, a large crowd gathered, including some relatives or friends of people attending the show. Despite the efforts by the police to restrain them, many broke through their lines, adding to the congestion outside the Iroquois.

The firefighters poured water on the fire, and within a relatively short time the fire was brought under control. Estimates varied on how long it took to extinguish the fire, ranging from as short as eight minutes to as long as 20 minutes. In the auditorium itself, the only combustible materials were the covers and fillings of the seats, a little wood, mainly on the doors and floors, and the carpeting and drapes. However, the highly combustible, numerous backdrops plus other material on the stage had fueled a terrible conflagration. Because a wire blocked the asbestos curtain, a curtain of dubious quality anyway, from being lowered, there was nothing to stop the flames. When a draft was created between the rear entrance doors of the stage and the gallery vents, the flames, accompanied by dark smoke, brought sudden death and desperate flight. That flight, given the large number of closed exits, the existence of dangerously placed steps, and the narrowness of some walkways, aisles, stairs, and platforms, had resulted in people being trampled and in people being trapped in twisted piles of fallen humanity.

In the end, the death toll would reach 602. Eddie Foy lived, escaping with only minor burns, and his son Bryan also survived. They were later immortalized in the

Hollywood movie *The Seven Little Foys*, starring Bob Hope as Eddie Foy. The Iroquois Theatre Fire is portrayed in the movie, but only briefly and with some inaccuracies.

No one was indicted on criminal charges, but damage claims were brought against the owners and managers of the Iroquois Theatre. In all damage trials the defendants were found to be "not guilty."

The Iroquois Theatre Building was repaired and refurbished. In less than a year, the new Oriental Theatre opened in the old Iroquois Theatre Building. Capacity crowds attended the initial performances at the Oriental.

Chapter 4

Cocoanut Grove Night Club Fire, November 28, 1942

The Cocoanut Grove Night Club originally opened on October 27, 1927, in an abandoned building of concrete and stucco in Boston, Massachusetts. The building, used previously as a garage and as a film exchange depot for Paramount Pictures, was remodeled into a night club with a distinctive decor. The interior, designed by noted night club architect Reuben Bodenhorn, simulated a tropical paradise. Dominating the interior were a number of large imitation coconut palm trees, with silver-tipped fronds.

The club did well at first. However, in the era of Prohibition, the Cocoanut Grove, unlike many of its competitors, refused to break the law and sell alcoholic drinks. Business declined.

In 1930, the Cocoanut Grove was sold to Charles "King" Solomon, a notorious bootlegger and racketeer. Solomon instituted changes. Liquor was served illegally, and high-priced performers of national stature appeared frequently. The Cocoanut Grove became the leading night club in Boston, a place frequented by the rich and famous.

On January 24, 1933, "King" Solomon was gunned down in the men's room of a nearby speak-easy called the Cotton Club. Shortly thereafter, Barnet Welansky, Solomon's attorney, acquired control of the Cocoanut Grove from Solomon's widow.

Prohibition was repealed in December 1933. Liquor was now served legally at the Cocoanut Grove. However, the Depression seriously hurt the night club business, and by 1935, Welansky was ready to sell the club. No one wanted to buy it. Welansky decided to keep the club open and to revitalize it. He refurbished the interior, upgraded the quality of the staff, and instituted a policy of booking promising local talent to entertain the patrons. The Cocoanut Grove prospered once more.

By 1938, business was so good that Welansky decided to expand. He bought the small building attached to the west side of the club and incorporated it into the Cocoanut Grove. The basement of the attached building was converted into a lounge, called the Melody Lounge.

The Melody Lounge was decorated in the same manner as the main floor. The furnishings included fish netting, rattan and bamboo trim, a dark blue satinlike material over the ceiling, leatherette covering much of the walls, and, of course, large imitation palm trees.

The Melody Lounge was dimly lit to provide a romantic atmosphere. There was indirect lighting over the large, enclosed octagonal bar in the center of the room. The only other lights were small 7 ½-watt bulbs interspersed among the fronds and coconuts of the palms. The electrical wiring for the Melody Lounge was installed by a man who did electrical work in his spare time. He was not a licensed electrician, as required by law, so he had not obtained the required installation permit.

By 1942, the Cocoanut Grove was amassing a net profit of about a quarter of a million dollars a year. Barnie Welansky decided to expand again. He acquired an adjoining three-story building to the east, connected it to the original building by an unobtrusive first-floor hallway, and remodeled the first floor of the newly acquired building into an additional lounge, the New Cocktail Lounge. The decor of the New Lounge was different from the rest of the Cocoanut Grove. The walls were covered in dark leatherette and hung with small oval mirrors. There was soft indirect lighting, installed by the same part-time electrician who had wired the Melody Lounge. Again the electrical work was done without a permit.

The New Lounge opened in mid-November 1942. Barnie Welansky could not be present for the opening. He was a patient in Massachusetts General Hospital, undergoing treatment for a heart ailment.

On November 20, 1942, Lieutenant Frank Linney, from the Fire Prevention Division of the Fire Department, inspected the Cocoanut Grove and filed his report. His evaluation of the New Lounge was as follows: "A new addition has been added on the Broadway side used as a cocktail lounge room, seating 100 people. No inflammable decoration" (Benzaquin, 1959, p. 188). His terse evaluation of the club as a whole included the following conclusions: "Sufficient number of exits. . . . Condition—Good" (Benzaquin, 1959, p. 188).

The configuration of the Cocoanut Grove on November 28, 1942, was, in part, due to the manner in which the two adjacent buildings had been joined to the original building. The main entrance was on Piedmont Street, at the south end of the club (see Figure 5a). You entered through a revolving door into a narrow foyer. In front of you was a checkroom and doors leading to a men's toilet and a ladies' powder room and toilet. To get to the Melody Lounge in the basement, you turned left, turned left again, and finally descended a steep, 4-foot-wide stairway. At the bottom of that stairway was the Melody Lounge. At the top of the stairs was an emergency exit onto Piedmont Street (see 1 on Figure 5a).

To enter the Main Dining Room from the foyer, you simply turned right and walked forward. In the center of the room was a dance floor flanked by seven tall, spectacular palm trees. Behind the dance floor at the east end of the room was an elevated bandstand. Tables surrounded the dance floor and bandstand.

Along the west and north walls of the room were elevated dining areas, set off by wrought-iron balustrades. The elevated terrace on the west was three feet above the main floor. The elevated terrace on the north side of the room was one step up. Behind the elevated north section, in the north wall, was an emergency exit, with two wings opening onto Shawmut Street (see 2 on Figure 5a).

On the south side of the Main Dining Room was an elliptical shaped bar, 48 feet long. This bar was called the Caricature Bar, because hanging there were caricature sketches of famous visitors to the Cocoanut Grove. Another bar was located along the south wall.

To the east of the bandstand on the north end of the Main Dining Room were some dressing and storage rooms plus a stairway (see 7 on Figure 5a) leading to more dressing rooms on the second and third floors. This area could be reached directly from the outside via two doors on Shawmut Street, a backstage exit door (see 4 on Figure 5a) and a performer's entrance (see 5 on Figure 5a). From the Main Dining Room, this area could be reached by doors behind the bandstand or by a doorway from the elevated north seating area (see 3 on Figure 5a).

The New Lounge, with its different decor, was set apart from the rest of the club. Entrance to the New Lounge was by a door on Broadway, not by the main entrance to the Cocoanut Grove. From the Broadway entrance, you passed through a small vestibule into the New Lounge via a single door that opened inward (see 8 on Figure 5a). There was a hallway with a right-angle turn running from the area of the Caricature Bar in the Main Dining Room to the New Lounge. However, there was no sign informing patrons of where that hallway went, and the hallway was dimly lighted. It was supposed to be closed off by a metal fireproof door, but the door had not arrived yet. Welansky was afraid that "deadbeats" would sneak out without paying, so he wanted the flow of people restricted both inside the club and when exiting. Consequently passage between the Main Dining Room and the New Lounge was to be limited, and a number of exterior doors were kept locked.

The kitchen, like the Melody Lounge, was in the basement. It was possible to go from the Melody Lounge to the kitchen, but the route was indirect and unmarked. You first had to exit the Melody Lounge via a concealed door (with no exit sign) on the north wall of the room (see Basement Plan, Figure 5b) into a narrow east-west corridor, with an emergency outside exit door down the corridor to your left and a door to the kitchen down the corridor to your right.

In the kitchen was a stairway leading up to the northwest corner of the Main Dining Room. To the east of the kitchen were large refrigerator units, storage rooms, and the furnace room (see Basement Plan, Figure 5b). At the east end of the furnace room was a narrow stairway leading up to the first floor.

On Saturday night, November 28, 1942, a fortuitous event would play a crucial role. Two young brothers from Brookline, Massachusetts, decided to go bar hopping in downtown Boston. The older brother, a 20-year-old defense worker, drove their black sedan. His younger brother was an 18-year-old college student. They tried to park in a parking garage, but all those nearby were full. They searched for a parking place on the street and lucked into one on Stuart Street, near Broadway. They locked the car and set off for the first of a series of bars.

At 10:15 P.M. that Saturday, a fire alarm came in from the call box at the corner of Carver and Stuart streets, in an area containing many hotels, theaters, and night

Figure 5a
Cocoanut Grove Night Club Street Floor Plan

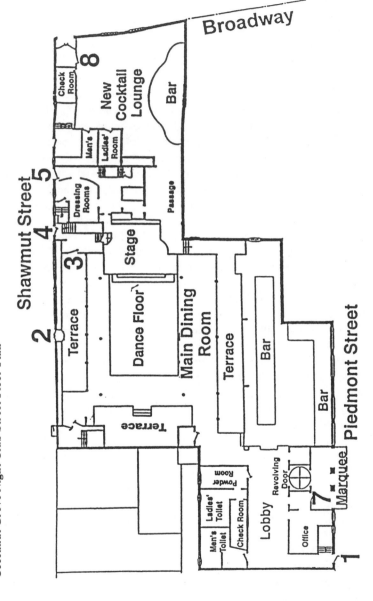

Reprinted with permission from *NFPA Journal*®, National Fire Protection Association, Quincy, MA 02269. *NFPA Journal*® is a registered trademark of the National Fire Protection Association, Inc.

Figure 5b
Cocoanut Grove Night Club Basement Plan

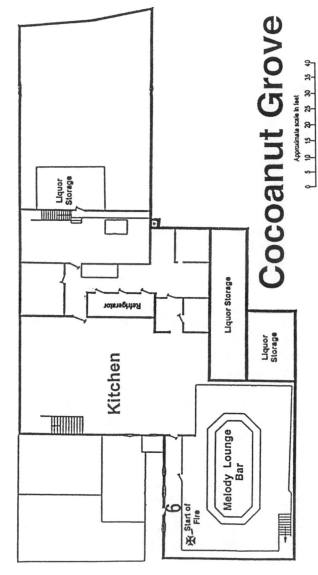

Cocoanut Grove

Approximate scale in feet

0 5 10 15 20 25 30 35 40

Liquor Storage

Refrigerator

Kitchen

Liquor Storage

Liquor Storage

Melody Lounge Bar

Start of Fire

Reprinted with permission from *NFPA Journal*®, National Fire Protection Association, Quincy, MA 02269. *NFPA Journal*® is a registered trademark of the National Fire Protection Association, Inc.

clubs. The fire department responded immediately. They found fire and smoke inside an empty black sedan parked on Stuart Street, near Broadway. The firefighters smashed the car windows, extinguished the fire, and tore out the smoldering front seat cushions.

No owner appeared, and no one admitted to turning in the fire alarm. Someone took down the license plate number. The firefighters loaded their gear back on their trucks and prepared to leave. It was about 10:20 P.M. However, they would not be returning in the near future to their station. As they were about to discover, just down the street from them the worst night club fire in American history was already in progress at the Cocoanut Grove. Because of the fire in the Brookline brothers' black sedan, firefighters were already on the scene.

Business was booming that Saturday evening at the Cocoanut Grove. True, a gala victory party honoring the Boston College football team had been canceled. That afternoon at Fenway Park, mighty Boston College, unbeaten and untied, seemingly headed for the Sugar Bowl, had played Holy Cross, which was finishing a mediocre season. This was a traditional season-ending rivalry between two Catholic schools from Massachusetts, but with Boston College competing for number one in the national football polls, the game took on added importance. The Holy Cross Crusaders, 4 to 1 underdogs, had upset the Boston College Eagles by the incredible score of 55–12, and so the Boston College celebration party that night at the Cocoanut Grove had been canceled. Holy Cross supporters did have a victory celebration that night, but not at the Cocoanut Grove.

Despite the cancellation, an overflow crowd of customers came to the Cocoanut Grove that night. By 10:00 P.M., all 100 tables in the Main Dining Room were occupied and additional tables were set up on the edges of the dance floor. At the Caricature Bar, the crowd was sometimes two or three deep.

Among those in the Main Dining Room was Hollywood cowboy star Buck Jones. Buck Jones, then 50 years old, had starred in many westerns. He was on a cross-country tour selling U.S. war bonds. Jones and his party were seated at a choice table on the terrace directly across from the bandstand.

The Melody Lounge in the basement was packed as well, with around 200 patrons enjoying drinks in the intimate atmosphere. All tables were taken, and people lined the bar, as many as four deep in spots.

A young man, in the Melody Lounge with his date, unscrewed one of the 7 ½-watt bulbs that were spaced among the fronds and coconuts of the palm trees. Presumably he and his date preferred complete darkness to the meager light provided by these bulbs. Stanley Tomaszewski, a 16-year-old high school student working weekends as a bar boy, noticed that the tiny light bulb had been unscrewed. He asked head bartender John Bradley what should be done. Bradley told him, "Go over and tell him nicely, you've got to put the light back on—it's the fire law" (Keyes, 1984, p. 26).

Tomaszewski, the bar boy, headed for the problem light, and the head bartender turned away. Tomaszewski explained to the couple seated on a settee that the light must be kept on. He then climbed on the settee and groped for the bulb. He turned the bulb the wrong way, and it came out. In the darkness, he could not find the socket among the palm fronds. In order to see where the socket was, he lit a match. After screwing the bulb back in, he blew out the match, dropped it to the floor, then stamped on it. The problem solved, Tomaszewski returned to the bar. It was about 10:05 P.M.

Behind him in the area he had just left, several people noticed a flicker of flames at the top of the palm tree. The top of the palm tree and the dark blue fabric covering the ceiling above it were on fire. Weekend cashier Daniel Weiss, a fourth-year medical school student at Boston University and the nephew of owner Barnet Welansky, noticed the fire and shouted to the bartenders to get water. Several bartenders and bar boy Tomaszewski fought the fire with towels, water, and seltzer, but when they put it out in one place, it appeared in another. Slowly it was spreading.

People at the northwest corner of the room where the fire was located (see Basement Plan, Figure 5b) were aware of the fire and the efforts to extinguish it, but few made an immediate effort to leave. Elsewhere in the Melody Lounge, people were unaware of the fire.

What originally seemed to be only a little fire, easily extinguished, now appeared to be a threatening one as it grew. A number of people close to the fire decided to leave.

Head bartender Bradley and bar boy Tomaszewski tried to haul down the burning tree in order to isolate the fire. Bradley finally succeeded in toppling the tree, but as it fell it glanced off his shoulder, burning him. Tomaszewski had successfully pulled down part of the flaming ceiling fabric, but the falling fabric burned his arms. Their efforts did not contain the fire. Suddenly the fire took off and raced across the ceiling fabric. Everyone in the Melody Lounge was now aware of the rapidly spreading fire.

Some 200 people were trapped in a windowless room with intense flames, thick smoke, and sizzling gases. All but a few employees knew of only one way out, up the narrow 4-foot-wide stairway to the emergency exit at the top, or beyond that, to the first floor foyer and the main entrance.

There was a rush to the stairs. Tables and chairs in the way were upended and pushed aside. People were knocked to the ground and stepped on. Some made it to the top of the stairs. The emergency exit door there was locked and could not be forced open, so they rushed onward to the front entrance. Behind them a giant ball of fire, accompanied by dense smoke and toxic fumes, roared up the stairway bringing death to those in its path. A pile of dead bodies blocked the stairs.

When the initial rush to the stairs occurred, Bradley shouted for people to use the exit door concealed in the north wall instead (see Basement Plan, Figure 5b). Tomaszewski and Bradley each led a group of patrons out by the concealed door. Then the electricity failed, plunging the room into darkness.

Once in the hallway north of the Melody Lounge, Bradley guided the people with him to the exterior door just down the hallway to the left (see 6 on Figure 5b). The exterior door was forced open, and they escaped into the alley north of the club. Tomaszewski, who had worked at the Cocoanut Grove only a few weekends, was unaware of the exit door in the corridor. He located a small window leading from the basement to Shawmut Street, and the people with him escaped through that window.

Those remaining alive in the Melody Lounge were quickly overcome by the deadly combination of dense smoke and toxic gases. Within a few minutes, everyone in the Melody Lounge was dead or unconscious with one exception—cashier Daniel Weiss.

Weiss, reluctant to abandon the money in the registers, hesitated inside the bar when the fire spread through the room and up the stairs. Finally he did move for the gate underneath the bar, but at that point the lights went out. In the darkness, on his hands and knees, Weiss crawled to the gate. He tried to push it open, but he could not. It would not yield, even when he drove his shoulder into it. Remembering that there was a bar sink next to the gate, he found a towel and soaked it with water from the partly full sink. He covered his face with the wet towel and lay on the floor. No one came to save him.

The fire seemed to have burned itself out, but the room was full of smoke and gas. Weiss resoaked the cloth and scrambled over the bar. He landed on a pile of dead bodies stacked against the bar gate. Fighting nausea, Weiss successfully located the concealed door leading toward the kitchen. Emerging through the door, he found himself in a dark hallway free of smoke and fire. He could breathe safely. Daniel Weiss was the last person to escape the Melody Lounge under his own power.

Although he had worked weekends at the Cocoanut Grove for a long time, Weiss did not know that down the hallway to his left was an exterior door. He knew of only one way out, the kitchen door to his right. Groping along in the darkness, he found that door and entered the kitchen. It was about 10:20 P.M.

Some people, unable to exit through the locked emergency door, headed for the main entrance door. As they reached the foyer, the ball of fire from the Melody Lounge exploded up the stairs, down the hall, and across the foyer.

The heat was intense. People's hair was singed. In a desperate effort to escape the fire ball, the fugitives from the Melody Lounge rushed for the revolving door. The fastest and most aggressive escaped alive. The rest did not.

Inside the Main Dining Room, people were disturbed by noise and shouting in the foyer. There were shouts from the foyer that sounded to some like "Fight!" As smoke infiltrated the room, the actual word being shouted became clear, "Fire!"

Black smoke poured into the Main Dining Room. Flames raced across the ceiling toward the ceiling vent above the Caricature Bar. The entire ceiling was ablaze, and the fire was descending the walls. Burning debris fell on people. The smoke and noxious gases were overpowering. Then the lights went out.

The patrons in the Main Dining Room knew of only one way out, the way they had entered, through the revolving door. However, hundreds of people were trying to exit there at the same time, and the foyer leading to the revolving door was aflame. Some tried to fight their way through the crowd and the flames to the front entrance. Others searched for another way out and found alternative exit paths.

Those on the north side of the room quickly discovered the concealed emergency exit in the north wall (see 2 on Figure 5a). It was locked. People banged into the double doors, and finally they burst open. Out came a wave of people. It was all people could do just to keep standing, as they were swept along with the outgoing tide.

The band, followed by a few others, exited behind the bandstand toward the backstage exit door onto Shawmut Street (see 4 on Figure 5a). Others reached the same exterior exit by heading through the interior door at the east end of the raised terrace seating section (see 3 on Figure 5a). The door onto Shawmut Street was locked. They were stymied.

Some discovered the unmarked hallway leading from the Caricature Bar to the New Lounge. They tried that means of egress, although few knew where the hallway led. A few people descended the stairs that went from the Main Dining Room to the kitchen in the basement. Some stopped in the kitchen. Others pushed on, looking for a way out.

Meanwhile, the foyer and main door had become clogged. People who had exited the Melody Lounge, customers waiting to be seated in the Main Dining Room, and patrons who had been in the Main Dining Room all tried to push through the narrow foyer and out the revolving door. Inevitably in the surging crowd, friends and relatives were parted.

Then the revolving door jammed, imprisoning those inside and bringing further egress to an end. The four people inside desperately heaved at the door. The door came free, hurtling them out. Then the door came off its framework and jammed again—this time for good.

The fire found its way across the foyer and reached the revolving door. Those trapped inside were burned to death. Those outside could do nothing to save them, but could only watch in horror through the glass door.

There was actually another way out of the building from the foyer area, albeit a small one. Inside the ladies' powder room was a casement window. Two women, strangers, happened to be in the powder room when the fire started. They heard someone yelling to get out and smelled smoke. One of them opened the window, and out they went, lowering themselves onto a parked car, and then to the alley below. As far as is known, no one else exited through that window.

While people in the Melody Lounge and in the Main Dining Room desperately tried to escape the conflagration, patrons and employees in the New Lounge were unaware of the disaster headed their way. Among those in the New Lounge were Jimmy Welansky, the younger brother of owner Barnie Welansky, Police Captain Joseph Buccigross, night commander of the district, and County Assistant District Attorney Garrett Byrne. With owner Barnie Welansky in the hospital with cardiac problems, Jimmy Welansky was nominally in charge. Jimmy had several of his own bars to manage, and he left operations at the Cocoanut Grove almost entirely to the regular staff. Welansky, Buccigross, and Byrne were together at a table near the dark, unmarked hallway that ran between the Caricature Bar and the New Lounge.

Suddenly a female employee ran toward them from that hallway. She gasped, "Mr. Welansky. There's a fire! . . . In there. Everywhere" (Keyes, 1984, p. 57).

They looked toward the hallway. Out of it came puffs of black smoke. Then a group of people raced wildly into the room from the hallway. Police Captain Buccigross tried to steady the group: "Hold up! Don't panic!" (Keyes, 1984, p. 57).

There was no stopping the fugitives from the holocaust of the Main Dining Room. They surged forward, knocking Buccigross down.

Behind the escapees from the Main Dining Room, driving them on, were dense black smoke and a plume of fire. Everyone in the New Lounge was now rushing away from the smoke and fire toward the Broadway door—too many people, too little time, too narrow an exit path, and an interior door that opened inward.

Assistant District Attorney Garrett Byrne and Jimmy Welansky were carried along by the frantic crowd and exited onto Broadway. Police Captain Buccigross climbed to his feet, and he too found himself propelled by the surging crowd out onto the sidewalk on Broadway. Unfortunately, people were pushed between the inner door (see 8 on Figure 5a) and the wall, and their efforts to extricate themselves partially closed the door. More people got pressed into the door by the inexorable force of those behind them. The door was being jammed closed.

Escape by the Broadway entrance became almost impossible due to the congestion at the nearly closed door. As fire further enveloped the room and the smoke became more stifling, people tried to break through glass blocks that formed part of one wall, but to no avail. It was just past 10:20 P.M.

At the same time, the firefighters who had extinguished the automobile fire on Stuart, near Broadway, were about to depart. One of them happened to glance down the street and saw smoke. Several ran down Stuart to Broadway, and saw that the New Lounge of the Cocoanut Grove was on fire.

The firefighters rushed into action. One man was sent to the nearest alarm box. He turned in an alarm to headquarters at 10:23 P.M. Actually, an earlier alarm had been sounded by someone at 10:20 P.M., so some companies were already in transit.

After sounding the alarm, the firefighter returned via Piedmont Street, encountering heavy smoke and flames coming from the front of the building. A number of severely injured people were lying on the sidewalk and in the street. Then he heard what sounded like an explosion from the rear. This was far worse than he had thought. He returned to the call box and turned in another alarm. It was 10:24 P.M.

Additional fire trucks were already arriving, and more were on the way. All would be needed, for the entire Cocoanut Grove Night Club was now ablaze.

Inside the Cocoanut Grove, people, safe for the moment from the advancing fire, had to make some difficult decisions. The people in the kitchen had first been alerted by a few employees and customers who had descended the stairs to the kitchen from the Main Dining Room. Several of these people had continued on toward the stairway in the basement beyond the furnace room (see Basement Plan, Figure 5b). Then Daniel Weiss, escaping from the Melody Lounge, entered from the basement hallway.

Weiss was dumbfounded to find in the kitchen about 25 people, some kitchen help and some customers, seemingly paralyzed with fear. Weiss scouted out the path to the stairs in the furnace room and found it to be clear. The others refused to leave the safety of the basement, which, though filling with smoke, was still free of fire. So Weiss alone mounted the stairs to the first floor. It was not yet 10:30 P.M.

Meanwhile, on the second and third floors, performers were dressing for the 10:30 P.M. show. They were warned by dining room assistant-headwaiter Charlie

Mikalonis, who, when the fire erupted into the Main Dining Room, escaped from that room and headed for the backstage exit door (see 4 on Figure 5a). It was locked, and despite the efforts of a number of people, could not be forced open. He headed for the performer's entrance (see 5 on Figure 5a). It was locked, too. At that point, Mikalonis rushed up the stairs to warn the performers on the floors above. He banged on the dressing rooms: "Get out, get out! The whole damn place is on fire!" (Keyes, 1984, p. 20).

Smoke was now coming up the stairs to the second floor. Below both doors onto Shawmut Street were locked, so Mikalonis decided to climb through a window onto the roof, hoping to climb down from there. The others had three choices: follow Mikalonis onto the roof; go down the stairs; stay where they were. Some opted for each choice.

By now it was about 10:30 P.M., and firefighters on the scene were doing what they could to rescue survivors and put out the fire. The narrowness of the streets around the Cocoanut Grove hampered the efforts of the ever-increasing number of fire companies arriving on the scene. Some fire trucks could get no closer than 150 yards, and the firefighters had to carry hoses, ladders, and axes the remaining distance. The police tried to hold back the growing number of media representatives and spectators, some of whom were genuinely interested in helping with the rescue attempts.

The first firefighters on the scene tried to enter the New Lounge from Broadway. At first the intensity of the fire kept them at bay, but soon they forced their way into the vestibule. The interior door was jammed closed by bodies pressed against it. A group of firefighters succeeded in forcing the door open. The firefighters, as quickly as possible, pulled people out, most of them dead.

On Shawmut Street, two locked exterior doors had been forced open from within, first the double doors from the Main Dining Room (see 2 on Figure 5a), and later, after initial failures, the backstage door (see 4 on Figure 5a). Shortly after people finally succeeded in breaking open the locked backstage door, Daniel Weiss reached the top of the stairs from the furnace room. He found people staggering through that door onto Shawmut Street, most of them suffering badly from burns, smoke inhalation, or gas poisoning. Weiss exited. Bodies lay on the sidewalk and in the street. He yelled at a firefighter, "There are people downstairs!" (Keyes, 1984, p. 57). It was just short of 10:30 P.M. on Weiss's watch.

Elsewhere on Shawmut Street, firefighters opened new escape paths. They broke through the performer's entrance on Shawmut Street (see 5 on Figure 5a). There were large plate glass windows on Shawmut Street. However, when the firefighters broke those windows, they found an interior wall behind the windows. The firefighters hacked through the interior wall, creating additional exit paths. For most of the victims of the fire, it was too late.

Firefighters, some equipped with oxygen masks, headed down the stairs to the furnace room. There was no fire in the basement, but the smoke was quite thick. The firefighters made their way from the furnace room to the kitchen. The floor was strewn with people. Many had covered their faces with towels or some other piece of material. Some were conscious. Some were unconscious, but still breathing.

Some were dead.

Inside the built-in refrigerator units were eight people. They had taken refuge there. Although cold and shivering, they were in good shape.

Firefighters evacuated the living from the furnace room and kitchen. Then they proceeded into the hallway north of the Melody Lounge. From there they entered the Melody Lounge. The dead were piled up near the exit door to the hallway. The dead were slumped over tables and draped over the bar. The dead lay on the floor. And worst of all, the dead were piled on top of one another on the stairs up to the foyer. The records of Boston City Hospital and Massachusetts General Hospital, the two hospitals receiving the vast majority of the victims, indicate that only two people in the Melody Lounge were still alive when the firefighters arrived, and both were unconscious.

The performers caught in the second- and third-floor dressing rooms when the fire raced through the building below them had split into three groups. Some, with assistant-headwaiter Mikalonis, went out on the roof. They either jumped down from there or were assisted down by firefighters with ladders. Some remained in the dressing rooms. Firefighters extended ladders up to them and rescued them. Some went down the dark stairway, through dense smoke, to the first floor. Fortunately, just as they reached the first floor, firefighters broke through the locked performer's entrance. Eyes burning, gasping for breath, they stumbled through the doorway onto Shawmut Street and safety.

On Piedmont Street the firefighters had difficulty entering the club. The revolving door had become dislodged from its track by the people trying to exit there, and it would not turn. The futile efforts of people to escape had broken the glass in places. Then the intensity of the heat had completely shattered the glass panels. The dead were piled up inside the doorway and had to be yanked free.

The firefighters discovered what had once been a door adjacent to the recessed main entrance. This locked metal door had no outside handle or knob. The firefighters pried it open with crowbars and found themselves inside the checkroom and office on the south side of the building, off the foyer (see 7 on Figure 5a). A portable clothes rack covered the door on the inside.

Eventually firefighters broke through the emergency exit at the top of the stairs to the Melody Lounge. To their right were the stairs covered with the bodies of those who had failed to reach the top in time.

On Piedmont Street, as on Shawmut Street, there were large plate glass windows. Again, behind these windows were interior walls. Just above ground level were small windows. These, also covered on the inside by an interior wall, opened onto the Melody Lounge.

By a little after 11:00 P.M., the fire was out in almost all of the Cocoanut Grove Night Club. Less than an hour had passed since the fire had begun in the Melody Lounge.

Hundreds of people lay on nearby sidewalks, gutters, and streets. Many were severely injured, others were dying or dead. Ambulatory victims milled about, some in pain, some hysterical, some searching for a companion or loved one.

The ever-increasing crowd of spectators, perhaps in the thousands, gradually swelled by friends or relatives of feared victims, pressed forward trying to breach the police lines. The cluttered streets impeded the evacuation of people to hospitals, but eventually the police opened clear routes. By about midnight, all victims of the fire had been transported away.

When the bar-hopping brothers returned to their car, they found the area cordoned off by the police. However, the police allowed them to go to their car and move it. When they reached the car, they were dismayed to find the windows broken and the front seat gone. They assumed that the damage was caused by vandals. Using a spare tire for a driver's seat, they were able to drive the car home. Several days later they would find out what had really happened. How the fire inside the car started would remain a mystery, but certainly that fire brought firemen to the Cocoanut Grove five to 10 minutes sooner, thereby saving the lives of perhaps 100 people.

Of the approximately 1,000 people inside the Cocoanut Grove that night, 492 died, including movie star Buck Jones. About 150 others received serious injuries. Some died of burns or damage to their lungs produced by heat, but most died from smoke inhalation, carbon monoxide poisoning, or acrolein poisoning. Acrolein, a toxic ingredient used in tear gas, was a chemical found in the leatherette, or imitation leather, used extensively on the walls and in the furnishings of the Cocoanut Grove.

A grand jury indicted 10 people, including: for manslaughter, Barnet Welansky, principal owner, and James Welansky, who was taking his brother's place on the night of the fire; for accessory after the fact of manslaughter and willful neglect of duty, Lieutenant Frank Linney, inspector for the Boston Fire Department; for willful and corrupt neglect of duty, Captain Joseph Buccigross, night commander, Division 4, of the Boston Police Department; and for conspiracy to violate building laws, Reuben Bodenhorn, architect and designer for the club, Samuel Rudnick, contractor and builder of the New Lounge, and David Gilbert, Rudnick's building foreman.

Of those indicted, two were convicted. Barnet Welansky, owner, was found guilty of manslaughter and was sentenced to 12 to 15 years at hard labor. Samuel Rudnick, builder of the New Lounge, was found guilty of conspiracy to violate building laws and sentenced to two years in prison, but his lawyer appealed, mainly arguing that since the other two alleged conspirators had been acquitted, the jury had found Rudnick guilty of a one-person conspiracy, a logical impossibility. The appeals court ruled that the verdict was proper, but given that only one of the alleged conspirators was found guilty, Rudnick's sentence should be suspended. So Rudnick did not go to prison.

Although all others were found not guilty, careers were damaged in some cases, principally that of Captain Joseph Buccigross. He was suspended without pay for 18 months pending his trial. In the summer of 1944, at the recommendation of the attorney general of Massachusetts, the charge against Buccigross was dropped. He eventually obtained his 18 months back pay, but he was never restored to a position of authority, working until retirement at a desk job in police headquarters.

Civil claims against the Cocoanut Grove originally totaled about $8 million, but were later reduced to about $2.5 million. However, there were few assets with which to pay claimants. Insurance policies carried by Welansky amounted to only $80,000.

The property was sold for $15,000. The largest source of revenue came from a discovery made after the fire. Firefighters, in sifting through the rubble for bodies, found a huge storage vault behind a wall in the Melody Lounge. The vault contained over 4,000 cases of liquor—whiskey, wine and beer—all unharmed by the fire. The liquor was auctioned off for $171,000. However, the federal government demanded from the estate unpaid taxes on the bottles of liquor, since none had federal tax stamps. Eventually, the federal government agreed to reduced duties of only $15,000. Then the Internal Revenue Service (IRS) demanded back payment of income taxes allegedly owed by Barnie Welansky. The IRS eventually settled the claim for a substantially reduced amount.

It took several years to resolve all claims against the Cocoanut Grove, and in the end, there were only enough assets to pay each claimant about five cents on each dollar claimed. It is estimated that on average each claimant received about $160.

Barnie Welansky was the only person indicted who went to prison. In June 1946, he was diagnosed with cancer of the right lung and trachea. He received radiation treatments at Massachusetts General Hospital, but his condition worsened. Clearly he would die in the near future. In November 1946, Governor Tobin, in consideration of Welansky's imminent death, granted him a pardon. As he left prison on November 26, 1946, Welansky told reporters: "I only wish I'd died then, with the others" (Keyes, 1984, p. 263). Early in 1947, Welansky died at age 50.

The investigation headed by Fire Commissioner William Arthur Reilly noted some of the major causes of loss of life: the locked doors; the unfamiliar location of most exits; the inaccessibility of the normal exits due to fire; the jamming of the revolving door; and the failure of the lighting system. The investigation concluded that: "this fire will be entered in the records of this department as being of unknown origin" (Benzaquin, 1959, p. 223). The evidence, it was stated, did not establish with certainty that Tomaszewski's match was the cause. Other possibilities, such as faulty electrical wiring, were investigated, but the exact cause could not be attributed to any specific cause or causes.

Perhaps the most important part of the report was the section on recommendations, because many of them were enacted into law, not just in Boston and Massachusetts, but throughout the country. There should be automatic sprinklers in every room. If a basement is a place of assembly, there should be at least two direct means of access to the street and a metal-covered automatic-closing fire door between the basement and the first floor. Exit doors should have panic locks and no others. Exits should be marked by "EXIT" signs, powered by a supplementary electrical system unaffected by a failure of the main system.

Chapter 5

Hartford Circus Fire, July 6, 1944

The afternoon of Thursday, July 6, 1944, in Hartford, Connecticut, was hot and sunny, with a breeze out of the west. The Ringling Brothers and Barnum & Bailey Circus had a matinee performance that day outside, under the big top.

The previous day the circus had been several hours late in arriving from a performance in Providence, Rhode Island. Consequently, the matinee performance on July 5 had to be canceled. When a building inspector from the Building Commission of Hartford had gone to the circus grounds at about 11:00 A.M. on July 5, the big top had not been set up yet. He returned at around 3:45 P.M. and spent roughly an hour inspecting the facilities. He "was satisfied that erection of tent, construction of seats and exits complied as in previous years" (Hickey, 1945, p. 5).

The Hartford Fire Department had no legal authority to inspect the circus grounds. In fact, the fire department was never officially notified that the circus was performing in Hartford.

The Hartford police chief assigned 55 officers to the performance. They were there primarily to control vehicle traffic and to provide protection against theft and vandalism. They were not there to help regulate pedestrian traffic, and none were stationed inside the big top.

The circus itself had limited fire-fighting equipment: 14 water pails, a few fire extinguishers, and four water trucks, used normally to dampen dust. There were no fire drills and no training in fire-fighting techniques.

The big top was aptly named. The giant tent was 425 feet long and 180 feet wide, encompassing over an acre and a half (see Figure 6). The seating capacity was 9,048. There were 6,048 reserved seats in four center sections, two on the north side and two on the south side. A substantial number of these seats were free-standing folding chairs. There were 3,000 general admission seats, in two sections at the west end and two sections at the east end. The stands in each section were 16 to 18 rows deep, about 10 ½ feet above ground level at the rear.

Figure 6
Hartford Circus Tent

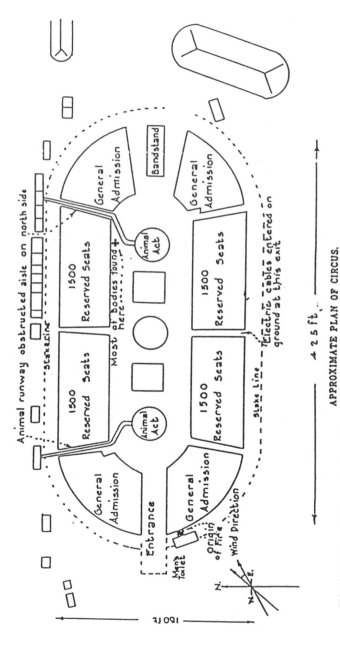

APPROXIMATE PLAN OF CIRCUS.

This plan, drawn after an examination of the ruins, shows the approximate arrangements, but may not be accurate in all details. The small squares beyond the side of the tent were animal cage wagons. Many other circus wagons in front of the main entrance and elsewhere on the grounds are not shown on this plan. At the right were performers' tents not involved in the fire.

Reprinted with permission from *NFPA Journal*®, National Fire Protection Association, Quincy, MA 02269. *NFPA Journal*® is a registered trademark of the National Fire Protection Association, Inc.

There were nine openings. The main entrance was on the west side of the tent. At its beginning under an outside canopy, the main entrance was 30 feet wide, but it narrowed to just over 20 feet wide at the inside between two general admission sections. At the far east end of the tent was a bandstand with openings on each side. Each of the openings on either side of the bandstand was 29 feet wide at the point of exit, but narrowed to just over 14 feet on the inside. The north and south sides of the tents both had three small exits, each 9 to10 feet wide on the inside and narrowing down to just over 5 feet at the point of exit. These exits were mainly for use by circus personnel, although the public had access to them. The center exit on the south side was used for running electric cables into the tent. The two side exit paths on the north side of the tent were obstructed by animal chutes when certain animal acts, such as those using big cats, were performing (see Photograph 2). These animal chutes were 3 to 4 feet high and 2 to 3 feet wide, and were enclosed by steel bars. Each was bridged by only one set of steps, 5 feet wide and five steps high. These animal runways connected the great steel-barred cages where the animals performed to their wagons outside.

Inside the center of the tent along the east-west axis were three show rings. Between each ring was a square platform. A metal railing separated the stands from the performance rings and platforms. The area between this railing and the rings and platforms was 26 to 27 feet deep at the narrowest point.

At the matinee performance on July 6, 1944, there were 6,789 paid admissions. Along with these ticket holders, a number of free admissions, including service men in uniform and purchasers of war bonds, and the employees of the circus brought the total inside to 7,500 to 8,000 people.

The third act was the Great Wallendas, one of the best high wire troupes ever. The Wallendas climbed rope ladders to the high wire above the center ring as Albert Court's animal act was finishing below them. At the conclusion of the animal act, the animals would be driven back to their cages through the two chutes.

As the animals were being driven out through the chutes, the spotlights focused on the Great Wallendas. Karl, Herman, and Yetta (Henrietta) Wallenda plus Joe Gieger were on one platform, and Helen Wallenda was on the opposite platform. They were in place, ready to begin. However, on this day, the Great Wallendas would not perform. It was 2:40 P.M., and disaster struck.

A fire, just a small fire, was observed by some people on the west side wall of the tent behind general admission Section A, near the main entrance (see Figure 6). Among those noticing the fire were three ushers, Kenneth Grinnell, Mike Dare, and Paul Runyon. They reacted quickly, getting buckets of water and heading for the fire, which initially seemed small enough to be extinguished by just a little water. Before they could reach the fire, the flames leaped upward in a large column. The heat of the flames scorched their clothes, forcing them to retreat.

When the fire broke out, a small group of Hartford police detectives happened to be at the main entrance searching for a parole violator whom they suspected might be a circus worker. Several of the officers later reported that they saw the fire early on but did nothing for fear of causing a panic.

The circus did not have access to the one established flame-retardant waterproof-

Photograph 2. Hartford Circus Animal Runway. The metal runways for big cats impeded the exiting of many, especially children, who had great difficulty getting over them. Note that the runway in the foreground comes almost to the waist of the man behind it.

ing solvent, because it was restricted to use by the military. In order to waterproof the canvas, they treated it with a mixture of paraffin thinned with gasoline. The mixture had been applied in April at the winter quarters of the circus in Florida. That coating, once ignited, would represent a major fire hazard.

Feeding on the paraffin and gasoline mixture, the fire spread with incredible quickness, according to witnesses, almost faster than the eye could follow. The entire tent was soon ablaze. The circus had inadequate fire-fighting equipment and inadequate personnel to combat a conflagration of this magnitude. For the people inside, it was a matter of getting out quickly or being burned alive (see Photograph 3).

According to Thomas Murphy, an editorial writer on *The Hartford Courant* who was there watching the show with his five-year-old son, the initial reaction of people around him was to exit in an orderly manner. He first became aware of the fire when he heard a woman gasp, "Look—fire" (Murphy, 1944, p. 11). He looked and saw a tiny tongue of flame creeping up the side wall of the tent near the main entrance. Others around him saw it also and rose to their feet. According to Murphy, at that moment several men shouted, "Take it easy. Take it easy. Walk out quietly" (Murphy, 1944, p. 11).

Did the crowd take it easy and walk out quietly? According to Murphy, "the crowd seemed to subside for an instant" (Murphy, 1944, p. 11). So perhaps they would have exited in an orderly manner if the fire had not spread so rapidly; but the entire tent was soon burning. Large pieces of canvas burned off and fell on the crowd, setting fire to the clothes and bodies of the people below. Some of the pieces that fell were large enough to cover a hundred or more people. There was no time to move easily, deliberately.

Accounts of the fire do not describe any organized attempt by circus personnel to effect an efficient exiting. The police on the scene tried to assist individuals in escaping, but the police were few in number. The people inside were mainly left to fend for themselves, with the burning tent collapsing over them, with the heat of the flames searing them, with limited exit paths of uneven widths, with steel-encased animal runs blocking the paths of many, with loose folding chairs in the way of those in reserved seating, and with people behind impatiently pressing forward—add to that the fact that many of those in attendance were small children.

The evacuation of the children proved to be especially difficult. If you were in an elevated seat in a grandstand, should you drop the child to the ground, where the child would be closer to exiting but on his/her own? Or should you keep the child with you? Some opted for each alternative. If your way was blocked by a steel animal runway and the child was too small to climb over it, what should you do? Thomas Murphy, *The Hartford Courant* writer, tossed his five-year-old son over the runway, then climbed over himself. Both escaped unharmed.

The separation of parents from their children often occurred in the rush to the exits, especially when there were a number of children for one adult to guide. Murphy reported the following incident, which occurred outside the tent after he and his son escaped: "I saw one woman standing moaning and say, 'My four children! My four children! Where are they?' Then she spied one coming to her, crying,

Photograph 3. Hartford Circus Fire. People ran away from the burning tent, thereby keeping the exits free of congestion, which is a problem that can occur in an emergency evacuation. UPI/Corbis-Bettman.

and she ran and threw her arms around him. Then another, then another. Finally she had all four, ages 6, 7, 8, and 9. They were all crying and embracing each other. The woman was shouting, 'Thank God! Thank God' " (Murphy, 1944, p. 11).

When the Wallendas, high above the crowd, saw the flames spread across the roof of the tent, they slid down the ropes. All but Helen Wallenda climbed to the top of one of the animal runways and scampered across the top, making it safely to the outside. For the acrobatic Wallendas, that was an easy physical feat; but for most others, especially young children, exiting over the top of the runways was not a realistic option.

The breeze blowing through the main entrance from west to east blew the fire to the back, where thousands were trying to exit. The fire consumed most of the stands, and they began to collapse.

The shouting and screaming of people, the roaring of the fire, and the crashing of the stands created a deafening sound—but the band played on. Merle Evans and his band loudly played "Stars and Stripes Forever," the traditional circus signal for an emergency, until the last of the six great center poles fell, bringing down the last remaining section of the burning tent on top of them. Miraculously, all the band members escaped alive. According to *The New York Times* report, so did all the circus performers and ushers.

People were screaming. Many pushed their way out, with little regard for those in front. As a result of the pushing, some were pinned against the animal runways, even stepped on if they fell.

Both Thomas Murphy and Helen Wallenda reported getting a limb caught momentarily between the bars of an animal runway. Fortunately, Murphy was able to extricate himself. Helen Wallenda was not.

Wallenda had attempted to climb up the steel bars of a chute, as her fellow troupe members had done, but each time she tried to climb, the press of people from behind crushed her against the bars. The surging crowd shoved her to the ground, and people trampled her when she attempted to rise. Then her leg was pushed between two bars, and she could not free it. Fortunately, her brother Phillip was in the bleachers during the performance. Helen's bright orange costume allowed Phillip to locate her. He charged through the mass of people, pulled her free, and rolled her under a canvas side wall.

Those separated from loved ones often made an effort to reenter the tent. The wall of flames deterred some. Others were physically restrained by roustabouts and other circus workers.

People escaped through the exits or under the tent side walls. Donald Anderson, a 13-year-old boy, was carrying a knife he used for whittling, and he slit the tent in several places, allowing hundreds to escape through these slits.

The initial fire alarms were sent in from different alarm boxes, two at 2:44 P.M. and a third at 2:45 P.M. A total of six alarms would be received by the Hartford Fire Department between 2:44 P.M. and 2:49 P.M.

State Police Commissioner Edward J. Hickey was at the circus that day with his seven nephews and two other children. After getting all the children out safely, Hickey radioed police headquarters from a Hartford police car. Then he turned his attention to organizing the rescue effort, including creating access lanes for ambulances and other vehicles to transport the injured to the city's hospitals.

The fire consumed the tent rapidly. Within six to 10 minutes, before the first fire engines arrived, the fire was over. All that was left were the charred remains of the circus—and the dead. According to the police, most of the dead were piled about the animal runways, especially the inside of the east runway (see Figure 6), in some places two or three deep. Their bodies and clothes were badly burned. The final death toll reached 169, some burned beyond recognition. About two-thirds of the dead were children. Of the remainder, most were women. The number injured is sometimes listed at 478, but that is probably the number needing emergency treatment at a hospital. It seems likely that the number injured was much larger than that.

The cause of the worst fire in circus history was never determined. There was speculation about a discarded cigarette or an electrical short, but no one saw how the fire actually started. In 1950, James Dale Segee, under arrest in Ohio at the time, confessed to committing four murders and setting numerous fires, including the Hartford Circus Fire. He had worked for Ringling Brothers in 1944, and he was in Hartford at the time of the fire. Nevertheless, Hartford authorities believed that there was not enough evidence against Segee, and he was not charged. The state of Ohio had him committed to a facility for the criminally insane. In later years, Segee recanted his confession about starting the Hartford Circus Fire.

Damage suits against the Ringling Brothers and Barnum & Bailey Circus listed, among others, the following deficiencies: (1) insufficient number of exits; (2) some exits were obstructed; (3) insufficient personnel on duty; (4) inadequate fire-fighting equipment; (5) usage of dangerous and combustible materials, specifically the tent. Criticism of the city focused on a number of shortcomings: (1) the failure of the city fire marshal to examine the circus premises; (2) the failure of the fire department to have emergency equipment positioned near the main entrance; (3) the failure of the building commission to do an adequate inspection; and (4) the failure of the police department to provide adequate crowd control.

The circus returned to Sarasota, Florida. They had no big top. They were facing a substantial number of law suits, with cash reserves of only about a half-million dollars and an insurance policy of a half-million dollars.

Six of the Ringling management were indicted for involuntary manslaughter. They would plead no contest, and, after legal appeals, five would receive prison terms of up to one year.

Within a month, the Ringling circus was performing again, eventually drawing large enthusiastic audiences. The circus used the outdoor stadiums of professional teams or schools.

There were more than 600 financial claims, which eventually were settled for about $4 million. It took all the profits up to December 1950 to settle all these claims.

In July of 1956, the Ringling circus announced that the use of tents was being abandoned, and it never performed under a big top again. The city of Hartford adopted very stringent safety and insurance requirements for itinerant performance companies, so stringent that recent outdoor tent circuses such as the Clyde Beatty-Cole Brothers Circus have bypassed Hartford.

Chapter 6

Beverly Hills Supper Club Fire, May 28, 1977

The Beverly Hills Supper Club was located in Southgate, Kentucky, a small munici-
pality across the Ohio River from Cincinnati. The lavishly decorated building was
advertised by its owners as the Beverly Hills Country Club and the Beverly Hills
"Showplace of the Nation."

In 1977, Beverly Hills was a large, multiroom structure, designed to accommodate
a number of different events simultaneously (see Figure 7). The first floor alone
had over 62,000 square feet. There was a small second floor on the south side of
the building and a half-basement under the front, or south, side.

The front entrance was covered by a canopy. After you entered through two
successive sets of double doors, you were in the foyer, with a checkroom to your
left. Then you passed through a short, narrow hallway, about 12 feet wide, with
a gift shop and then stairs to the basement on your left and restrooms on your right.
From this hallway you entered into the Main Bar, billed as the Directoire Lounge.
In the middle of the room was a large oval bar.

To the left of the Main Bar Room was the Main Dining Room, also called the
Café Room, but advertised as the Café Frontenac. To the right of the Main Bar
were curtains covering a set of double doors, one entrance to a 30-foot-by-15-foot
room called the Zebra Room. Between the curtains and the double doors was a
cubbyhole housing the reservationist, who handled telephone reservations. Past the
curtains to your right was the open entrance to the Hallway of Mirrors. As you
entered the Hallway of Mirrors from the Main Bar, a wall of mirrors was on your
left and a spiral staircase leading to the second floor was on your right. Overhang-
ing the open spiral staircase, known as the Cinderella Stairway, was a huge crystal
chandelier, and beneath it was a small pool. Just beyond the spiral staircase was
the second, and primary, entrance to the Zebra Room, a set of double doors.

As you proceeded forward out of the Hallway of Mirrors, you stepped down into
the long North-South Corridor, running from the front of the building all the way
to the two main rooms in the back, the Cabaret Room and the Garden Room. After

Figure 7
Beverly Hills Supper Club

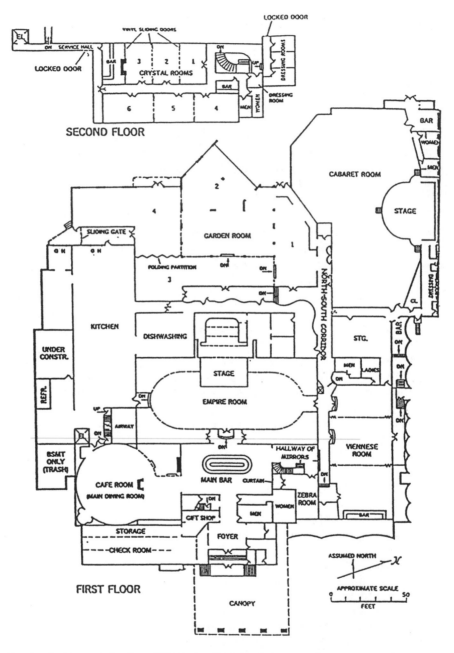

SECOND FLOOR

FIRST FLOOR

you stepped down into the North-South Corridor, you turned left and advanced toward the back of the building. On your right, you passed several entrances to the Viennese Room, a large room that could be partitioned into two or three separate rooms. Across the hall from the second entrance to the Viennese Room was an entrance on your left to a very large rectangular room, the Empire Room. The Empire Room was behind the Hallway of Mirrors, the Main Bar, and in part, behind the Main Dining Room. The Empire Room had one entrance from the North-South Corridor, a second entrance connecting the room to the kitchen, and a third entrance from the rear of the Main Bar Room.

As you moved further down the North-South Corridor beyond the Viennese Room on your right and the Empire Room on your left, you passed restrooms on your right, then came a corridor leading to your right and two adjacent corridors leading to your left. The corridor to your right had an entrance door that was camouflaged to blend into the wood paneling of the walls, and it ran along the south side of the Cabaret Room to the backstage dressing rooms. The first corridor to your left, accessed through a set of double doors, curved behind the Empire Room to the kitchen. The second corridor to your left curved behind the Garden Room, with three doors leading into the Garden Room. Along the length of these two corridors were several doors, allowing passage from one corridor into the other.

At the end of the North-South Corridor you came to the entrance to the Cabaret Room on your right and then the Garden Room on your left. For shows in the Cabaret Room, people were seated at a complex pattern of tables, arranged over four different levels below the stage (see Figure 8 and Photograph 4). The Cabaret Room also contained bars, restrooms, dressing rooms, dishwashing facilities, space for cashiers, and a storage closet. Famous entertainers performed in the Cabaret Room to crowds that sometimes exceeded a thousand.

The Garden Room to the left of the North-South Corridor was a large room with a glass back wall. It could be partitioned into as many as four different rooms. At the rear of the Garden Room were doors leading outside to a garden, gazebo, and chapel.

On the left, or west, side of the first floor was the large kitchen. The kitchen had separate doorways leading to the Main Dining Room, the Empire Room, and the Garden Room, so food could be brought directly from the kitchen to those rooms. An area to the west of the kitchen was under construction.

If you ascended the spiral staircase in the Hallway of Mirrors, you came to a fairly small second floor, which contained dressing rooms, restrooms, bars, and the Crystal Rooms. The Crystal Rooms, if all sliding doors were in place, consisted of a complex of six rooms, three on each side of an east-west hallway. If all the sliding doors were open, there were two long rectangular rooms, one on either side of the hallway.

The configuration of rooms, hallways, and exits that existed in 1977 was considerably altered from what it had been when the 4-R Corporation bought the club on December 30, 1969. A much smaller facility had been built in 1937, and over the years a number of owners had operated a night club and dining facility there, sometimes successfully and sometimes unsuccessfully. The four Rs, father Richard

Figure 8
Beverly Hills Cabaret Room

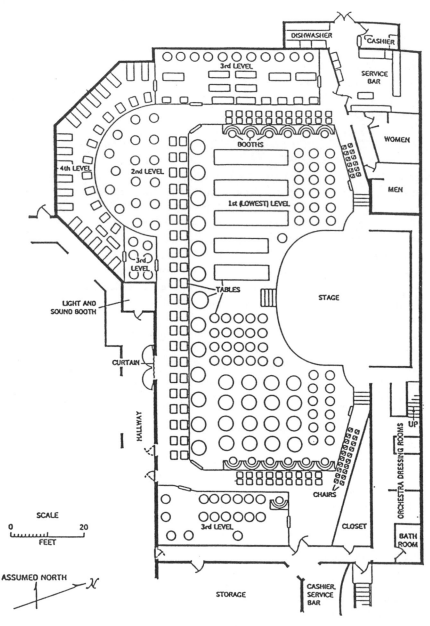

60

Photograph 4. Beverly Hills Supper Club Cabaret Room. This view is looking from the left rear to the right front of the room. The high density of unattached tables and chairs slowed egress from the overcrowded room. Reprinted with permission from *NFPA Journal®*, National Fire Protection Association, Quincy, MA 02269. *NFPA Journal®* is a registered trademark of the National Fire Protection Association, Inc.

(Dick) Schilling, Sr., and his three young sons, Richard, Jr. (Rick), Ronald (Ron), and Raymond (Scott), acquired the property after the previous owners had failed. Dick Schilling, Sr., and his sons made the club into a thriving business, and over the years, they expanded the club greatly.

There had been a fire at the Beverly Hills not long after Dick Schilling and his sons became the owners. Around 3:15 A.M. on June 21, 1970, a fire was reported there. The volunteer fire department of Southgate plus other departments from northern Kentucky eventually brought the fire under control, but much of the Beverly Hills had been destroyed. There was some evidence suggesting arson, but the arson investigation did not establish a definite cause.

Dick Schilling set out to rebuild the Beverly Hills. He wanted a bigger, more sumptuous supper club. The restored and enlarged Beverly Hills was similar to the club as it would exist in 1977 except that the forerunners of the Cabaret Room and the Garden Room were much smaller. On February 10, 1971, it reopened.

On February 26, 1971, *The Cincinnati Enquirer* ran a story under the headlines "Beverly Hills Supper Club a Safety Risk, Says State." The story reported that the building had not received approval for occupancy by the state fire marshal's office and that the Beverly Hills had opened without remedying 10 major safety defects identified by the state. Among the problems listed were the possible inadequacy of the exits, uncertainty regarding the use of suitable flame-resistant materials in the interior finish, and the presence of an unenclosed stairway, the open spiral staircase. Enclosed, fire-protected stairways restrict the spread of fire from one floor to another and provide a safe passageway. Following the story, the city fire chief Ray Muenchand and the state fire marshal John Calvert maintained that there were no major violations and that the owner was attempting to comply with all regulations. Nevertheless, a Campbell County, Kentucky, grand jury was convened to conduct an investigation of Beverly Hills. Its conclusion seemed to dispel any doubts about the safety of Beverly Hills:

We heard testimony from the state and local fire officials and are satisfied that Beverly Hills has complied with all fire and safety regulations. Frequent visits to this establishment are made by the Southgate Fire Department. We have been informed that the operators of Beverly Hills will train their employees in fire prevention and fire fighting in order to have its own "fire brigade," as soon as the employment situation stabilizes. (Lawson, 1984, p. 27)

The 1970–71 reconstruction had created a showroom, called the Cabaret Room, that could seat about 350 people. That showroom soon proved to be inadequate. Eventually Dick Schilling decided to enlarge the showroom, so that it could accommodate a thousand people. Schilling had a draftsman from a Cincinnati architectural firm draw the plans and acted as his own general contractor. In the last half of 1974, the Cabaret Room was expanded to about double its previous size, with an intended seating capacity of triple the prior capacity. It was a very large room with four different levels around a central stage. Despite the doubling in size and tripling in capacity, there was no increase in either the number of exits, three, or the width of the exits. Given the square footage of floor space and its intended usage, the capacity of the new Cabaret Room, according to building and fire codes, should have been a little over 500, not over 1,000.

In the spring of 1975, Dick Schilling remodeled the Zebra Room. He personally redesigned the room and supervised all construction. The electrical wiring was not placed in a metal conduit, and it was, therefore, in violation of the state electrical code. That same violation had occurred in the prior expansion of the Cabaret Room.

In the spring and summer of 1976, the room at the center-rear of the club was expanded into the Garden Room. The expansion increased the seating capacity to about 600. Again, Dick Schilling acted as his own general contractor.

The original expansion plans for the Garden Room called for the existing outside door near the north end of the North-South Corridor to be eliminated. The North-South Corridor would come to a dead end at the Cabaret Room. However, at the urging of the Southgate building inspector Richard Baiting and the state fire marshal's field inspector John Bramlage, Schilling agreed to extend the corridor to the rear of the building, where there would be exterior exits.

The remodeling had created serious pedestrian traffic-flow problems, especially when a large crowd exited the Cabaret Room. Not everyone was oblivious to the problem with the Cabaret Room. A state senator from Kentucky, Tom Easterly, attended a show in the Cabaret Room and noted that after the performance it took him more than 20 minutes to get out of the showroom and another 10 to 15 minutes to get through the North-South Corridor to the front of the building. He went to the state fire marshal's office and urged that the building be inspected. According to that state senator's account, the fire marshal admitted that the building constituted a fire hazard. Following the visit by the state senator, the fire marshal did order an inspection. On January 27, 1977, the field inspector Bramlage performed a cursory inspection when the building was unoccupied and concluded: "I will agree that patrons going out the front door to obtain automobiles would have some congestion, but in case of emergency, evacuation should be no problem with existing exits" (Dunn, 1979, p. 55).

On Saturday night, May 28, 1977, business was brisk. In the Cabaret Room, the singer John Davidson would give two performances to above capacity audiences of over 1,000 people per performance. Many of these people had dinner reservations at the club before the show. They would be served either before the first show in the Cabaret Room itself or in two other rooms, the Main Dining Room (the Café Room) and the Garden Room.

A number of special events would be occurring in various rooms throughout the club. On the first floor, four different events were scheduled. In the Empire Room, there would be 400 or more at the annual awards banquet and dance of the Greater Cincinnati Savings and Loan Association. The Viennese Room was divided by a partition, one section for a bar mitzvah celebration of just under 100 people and the other section for a small, private dinner party given by a local physician for some colleagues and their spouses. In the Zebra Room, there would be a 5:00 P.M. wedding reception and dinner for a party of about 25. The wedding itself would take place at 4:00 P.M. in the separate chapel located behind the supper club. Later in the evening another wedding party, of about 50, after a wedding outside in the garden, would be served dinner in a partitioned-off section of the Garden Room. In addition to people attending those affairs, there would be people coming just for dinner in the Café Room or Garden Room and for drinks at the Main Bar.

Upstairs, two special events, with about 120 people each, were scheduled. In the Crystal Rooms on one side of the hallway, the Greater Cincinnati Choral Union was holding a dinner, fashion show, and dance, and in the Crystal Rooms on the other side of the hallway, a banquet was scheduled for the officials and competitors of a dog show.

It was a warm, clear day. The balmy evening was going to be a busy one at the Beverly Hills. Dick Schilling was in Florida recuperating from surgery, so his three sons were in charge that night.

The first scheduled event was the wedding in the chapel, followed by cocktails and dinner in the Zebra Room. The last of the wedding party and guests left the Zebra Room at sometime between 8:00 P.M. and 8:30 P.M.

People at that wedding reception heard some unusual sounds four or five times, lasting several seconds each time. They were described by some as sounding like thunder and by others as a grinding sound, reminiscent of the sound made when moving furniture. The temperature in part of the room became uncomfortably hot. Guests asked the waitress, Shirley Baker, to turn up the air conditioning, but she said that it was already as high as it could go. While part of the room was quite cool, elsewhere the heat seemed to increase. One of the wedding guests reported afterward that he and his wife, while standing in the parking lot, noticed several puffs of black smoke coming from the roof. He looked at his watch, and it was 8:24 P.M. He suggested to his wife that it was probably just exhaust from an incinerator or the kitchen.

The now empty Zebra Room would not be used for the remainder of the evening. The waitress placed all the dishes on carrying trays, put out the candles, and left the room. The waitress returned a few minutes later to see if a busboy had removed the carrying trays. The trays were still there. She noted that portions of the room continued to be quite hot. As she exited in search of a busboy, she heard a buzzing in the lights.

The waitress found a busboy, and he entered the Zebra Room to remove the trays. While he was in the room, the ceiling lights flickered five or six times. Neither the waitress nor the busboy were alarmed by the heat or the irregularities with the lights.

Later, a cleaning woman, Manilla Poer, entered the Zebra Room to store a sweeper. She encountered nothing unusual and turned off the lights as she left. The cleaning woman then went to the women's restroom adjacent to the Zebra Room. A couple of women there expressed concern about the smell of smoke. The cleaning woman assumed that it was probably from a lighted cigarette that had been tossed into a wastebasket somewhere.

The female reservationist, Eileen Druckman, sat in the cubbyhole between the curtains and the west entrance to the Zebra Room (see Figure 9). Shortly before 9:00 P.M., she smelled smoke coming from the Zebra Room. She opened the doors to the Zebra Room and encountered gray, billowing smoke that stung her eyes. The

Figure 9
Beverly Hills Zebra Room

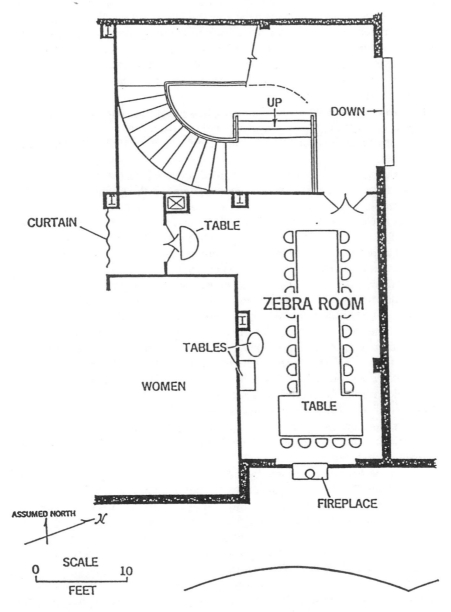

UP

DOWN →

CURTAIN

TABLE

ZEBRA ROOM

TABLES

WOMEN

TABLE

FIREPLACE

ASSUMED NORTH

SCALE

0   10

FEET

heat was intense and singed her hair slightly. She closed the door and immediately went to the front desk, located just past the foyer and inside the Main Bar.

The front desk was being handled by Marjorie Schilling, the wife of Rick. The reservationist informed her and a host who was there, Jim King, of the fire. The host ran into the cubbyhole, opened the door, and then quickly closed it as he too encountered heavy smoke. He hurried back to the desk and confirmed that the Zebra Room was on fire. Marjorie Schilling sent a hostess to find Rick, Ron, and Scott Schilling. She called the Southgate Police Department and then the fire department. At 9:01 P.M., the Southgate Volunteer Fire Department received the fire alarm from Beverly Hills.

The reservationist went to the Main Bar and told the head bartender of the fire. The head bartender got a fire extinguisher and entered the cubbyhole. The smoke was very dense, so he concluded that the fire was too great to fight with a fire extinguisher.

About the same time as the reservationist discovered the fire, two sisters who were waitresses for the bar mitzvah celebration dinner in the Viennese Room went to get some serving trays in the Zebra Room. As they went up the step from the North-South Corridor into the Hallway of Mirrors, the Main Bar was in front of them across the Hallway of Mirrors. They noticed some light gray smoke over the bar about a foot from the ceiling, but customers and workers in the bar seemed oblivious. At the entrance to the Zebra Room, one of the sisters turned the door-knob and opened the door. Black smoke poured out from the Zebra Room into the Hallway of Mirrors. She closed the door, left her sister there, and went in search of Rick or Ron Schilling, the two older brothers. Neither was in the Main Bar. She told one of the bartenders to call the fire department and headed for the kitchen.

Few people in the Main Bar had heard or even noticed either the reservationist or the waitress. Those who were aware of the smoke assumed that it was caused by a small fire that would be extinguished easily. Heavier and darker smoke began to come down from the light fixture and the ceiling vents. The need to evacuate become clear to patrons and employees alike. Patrons, on their own initiative, headed for the front doors. Employees urged people to remain calm and leave in an orderly manner. The customers in the Main Bar, about 50 to 100 people, were the first to exit the club.

Word of the fire spread informally throughout the club among employees and patrons. When Rick Schilling, the oldest brother, got news of the fire, he rushed to the Zebra Room door, still guarded by the waitress. Smoke was leaking into the corridor. He opened the door. No fire was visible, but heavy, black smoke poured out. He yelled, "Call the fire department and get everybody out!" (Lawson, 1984, p. 106). Then he ran toward the Main Bar, followed by the waitress who had previously guarded the Zebra Room door.

A woman on the second floor at the top of the spiral stairway observed Schilling's actions below her and spread the alarm to the Choral Union group upstairs. They began to exit down the spiral staircase.

Before Rick Schilling arrived at the Main Bar, employees there had decided to alert the Savings and Loan Association people inside the Empire Room, the room behind the Main Bar. When the large crowd in the Empire Room was informed of the fire and told to leave calmly, they did so. The people began to exit, but without haste. There was no smoke at that time in the Empire Room.

Meanwhile, people eating in the Main Dining Room had become aware of the smoke. They also started for the Main Bar and the front door.

A busboy informed people in the Viennese Room about the fire. There was no evidence of smoke or fire, but people slowly exited into the North-South Corridor, and then into the Hallway of Mirrors, heading toward the Main Bar.

Interestingly, there was an exit door on the east side of the Viennese Room. That door led to a concrete platform between the original outside wall of the building and a new outer facade that had been built along the east side of the supper club. From the platform, there were steps leading to outside double doors (see C on Figure 10). However, the east wall of the Viennese Room had curtains arranged to simulate window curtains, and those curtains covered the door. Although there was an exit sign over the door, some employees were unaware of its existence. No employee or patron used that exit. Afterward a chain and padlock were found attached to one of the double doors, but it could not be determined if the chain had been fastened to the second door, thereby locking it.

People from the Main Dining Room, Empire Room, and Viennese Room on the first floor and the Crystal Rooms on the second floor were all headed for one exit, the front entrance (see D on Figure 10). Between the Main Bar and safety outside was a short hallway, about 12 feet wide, and two successive double doors. A large number of people had to funnel through that narrow opening, and the flow of people became agonizingly slow.

An employee spread word of the fire to the Garden Room. At the time, there was no evidence of a fire there, but people began to exit through two sets of rear doors that opened directly outside (see F and G on Figure 10).

There were people lined up in the North-South Corridor, waiting to be seated for either dinner in the Garden Room or the show in the Cabaret Room. Those people were ushered out of the building through the exits at the rear of the Garden Room. The single door at the end of the corridor was locked (see H on Figure 10), but the double doors next to the single door were open (see G on Figure 10).

Outside, at both the front and back, congestion developed because people were slow to move away from the exit doors. Inside, most were moving toward an exterior exit, either the front entrance or the doors at the back of the Garden Room.

In the Cabaret Room, however, people continued to watch the show. Two comedians, Teter and McDonald, the warm-up act, were telling jokes to an audience that was unaware of the danger. John Davidson was in his dressing room, waiting to go on.

A busboy, Walter Bailey, had slipped off to the Cabaret Room to catch the comedians, but he had been detected there by Ron Schilling, who sent him back to work. As the busboy passed the Zebra Room, he became aware of the fire and the evacuation under way in the front of the club. He returned to the Cabaret Room. Dick Schilling's brother-in-law was working outside the rear doors, checking people's names against the reservation list and controlling the flow of people from

Figure 10
Beverly Hills Exits

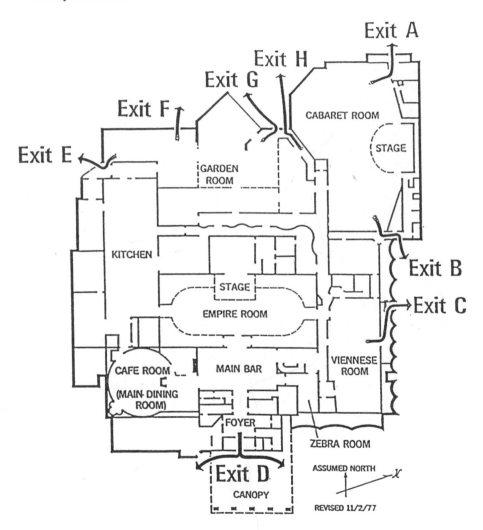

the corridor into the Cabaret Room. The busboy whispered to the brother-in-law that there was a fire in the Zebra Room. He decided that he should check the exterior doors behind the small bar room at the left, back corner of the Cabaret Room to make sure those doors were unlocked. He set off across the Cabaret Room for those doors without informing the audience about the fire.

The comedians continued their act. The audience sat there. The busboy stood alone at the back of the room. A minute or two passed.

It was 9:08 P.M. The 18-year-old busboy Walter Bailey decided to act on his own initiative. He walked purposefully across the middle of the floor, climbed onto the stage, and took a microphone from one of the comedians. He was tense and perspiring heavily, but he tried to sound calm when he spoke:

Turn around and look toward the back of the room. You will see a green exit sign. Notice it. Look to the corners of the room off to my left and right. There are other exit signs there. Notice them also. I want the left side of the room to go to this exit (pointing to left of stage) and the right side of the room to go to this exit (pointing to right of stage). There is a small fire on the other side of the building. There is no reason to panic or rush but you must leave. (Lawson, 1984, p. 126)

Some thought that he was a part of the act, but his seriousness seemed to impress most. Nevertheless, with the absence of any overt signs of fire, many were slow to move and some even remained seated. When the busboy reached the rear door, he saw that some were still sitting. He jumped on a couch and yelled for people to leave. The comedians on stage took the microphone, told people that there apparently was a small fire and that they should leave the building, but that once it was extinguished, they could return and the show would resume. The evacuation of the Cabaret Room was under way, but slowly.

Beverly Hills had no sprinkler system. Many employees had no knowledge about the location of fire extinguishers, and there had been no training in fire fighting, contrary to what a grand jury had been told in 1971. Consequently, response was slow and when it did come, dangerously inappropriate.

Two busboys who were in the kitchen when word of the fire spread to that room ran to the Zebra Room. When they reached the Zebra Room, it was unguarded. The doors were closed, but smoke was escaping from around the doors. One of the busboys touched a doorknob and found it to be extremely hot. A cardinal rule in dealing with fire is never open a door that feels hot, but the other busboy, in order to learn the severity of the fire, kicked open the door. The heat was intense. Smoke billowed out and then up the spiral staircase. One of the busboys ran for the kitchen to get a fire extinguisher. The other tried to shut the door but failed to close it completely.

Meanwhile, Ronald and Scott Schilling, the middle and youngest brothers, had gotten word of the fire. The two of them plus a bartender got fire extinguishers and hurried to the Zebra Room. When they arrived, one of the doors was open about 6 inches and black smoke was pouring out at the top. The room was hot and filled with smoke. The three men emptied their fire extinguishers into the room in the direction of what seemed to be a glow. The black smoke kept coming. Suddenly there was a loud rush of air and an explosion. The three men were blown into the Hallway of Mirrors. Flashover had occurred. Everything in the Zebra Room that was flammable had ignited simultaneously.

The fire exploded out of the Zebra Room, crossed the Hallway of Mirrors, and reached the far wall. It then spread in three different directions: down the Hallway of Mirrors to the Main Bar, up the spiral stairway to the second floor, and into the North-South Corridor. Fire spread rapidly along the top of the paneled walls and along the carpeted floors, with dark black smoke and noxious gases preceding it.

Heavy black smoke billowed up through the open spiral stairway. Fire began to move up the stairs. Some people were screaming and shouting. People in the rear were pushing. Two women tripped on the steps and fell. People stepped over them or on them in an effort to escape before the staircase became impassable. Some busboys helped the two women to their feet. Soon the entire stairway was on fire. People on the stairs were forced to retreat back to the second floor. All, including the two who had fallen, escaped the advancing flames. Those who were suffering most from the dense smoke and toxic gases received assistance from others.

The people attending the two events on the second floor knew of only one escape route, the spiral stairway. However, there was a second stairway. A service stairway at the opposite end of the hall from the spiral stairway connected the kitchen with the second floor. The manager of a dance band scheduled to play at the Choral Union party had used the elevator near that service stairway to bring up equipment. He had noticed the narrow wooden stairway, and now recalled it. He shouted to people that there was another way out, but only a few paid any attention to him. A small group did follow the band manager through the cloud of smoke and down the service stairway into the kitchen.

People in the kitchen had been warned, but there was no evidence there of the fire. Many employees were still preparing food. The band manager yelled at them: "Look, you goddamned fools, the building is on fire! How in the hell do you get out of here?" (Lawson, 1984, p. 138). They pointed to several doors but both were locked. He located an unlocked door at the back of the kitchen and then another that led outside (see E on Figure 10). He and the small group with him were safe.

The headwaiter of the Crystal Rooms and the other employees working there also knew of the service stairway. In addition, the headwaiter was aware of a door leading from the upstairs corridor to the roof, but it was locked. Despite the aid of several large patrons, it could not be forced open. The service stairway to the kitchen was the only open avenue of escape.

The lights on the second floor went out, then on again, then off for good. In total darkness, on hands and knees to get below the dense smoke, with eyes and throats burning, gasping desperately for breath, people crawled along the hall and then proceeded down the service stairway to the kitchen. Miraculously, all on the second floor made it to the kitchen, where the smoke was still thin, and from there out exits at the rear of the building (see E and F on Figure 10).

The smoke and fire spread into the Main Bar in force, turning what had been a relatively leisurely evacuation for people there into a nightmare. Most from the

Main Bar and Main Dining Room had exited while the smoke was still sparse, but evacuation of the Empire Room had occurred later. Many from the Empire Room had exited through the double doors to the Main Bar. They were on their way out when the smoke and fire rushed into the Main Bar from the Hallway of Mirrors. The bar itself was soon ablaze. Some shouted for people to get down, crawl, keep calm. Some screamed, one woman hysterically; but calmer people soothed agitated ones and helped them to keep going. Earlier there had been congestion in the foyer, but now traffic flowed quickly. In about three minutes all those still in the front had crawled to safety.

Meanwhile, Ron Schilling, knocked to the floor outside the Zebra Room when the fire erupted into the Hallway of Mirrors, scrambled to his feet and made for the Empire Room doors behind the Main Bar room. He told employees to send those still in the Empire Room out the back via the kitchen, not out the front door. Then he left, heading ultimately for the service stairway and the second floor. Employees in the Empire Room closed the doors to the Main Bar and directed the remaining people toward the kitchen. Some people exited instead at the opposite side of the room into the North-South Corridor. The Empire Room was still free of noticeable smoke. The evacuation was orderly and unhurried.

The kitchen had become a viaduct. People from the Cincinnati Choral Union and the dog show group on the second floor escaped down the service stairway and through the kitchen. People from the Greater Cincinnati Savings and Loan Association escaped from the Empire Room through the kitchen. Some of the party of physicians in the rear part of the Viennese Room were directed by a busboy through the Empire Room into the kitchen, and they escaped from there.

Dense smoke then infiltrated the kitchen. People took advantage of water there to wet a towel, handkerchief, or some piece of material and hold it over their faces.

Although there had been some very harrowing moments when death seemed imminent to some, everyone in the Main Dining Room, Main Bar, Empire Room, Viennese Room, and kitchen (all on the first floor) and everyone on the second floor exited the building alive. However, two decided to reenter. Two young women, who were coordinating the fashion show for the Choral Union party, had left money in an upstairs dressing room. They decided to reenter and went back inside through the kitchen. Afterward they were found in an upstairs dressing room, dead of smoke inhalation. Over 1,000 escaped from the front half of the building. Two died, foolishly.

The Garden Room had doors leading directly outside (see F and G on Figure 10). The relatively small number of people there exited easily. Others also exited through the Garden Room from the North-South Corridor and from the kitchen.

The Cabaret Room began to yield its 1,000 plus customers. Those who went out the rear doors were directed out via the Garden Room in the back. Employees tried to hurry people along, but exiting from the Garden Room slowed somewhat. For those still in the North-South Corridor, horror was on its way.

Heavy black smoke and fire began to move up the North-South Corridor. Those in its path were forced to drop down in order to breathe. Visible fire rolled quickly down the hallway, along the ceiling, and along the carpet.

Three waitresses were trapped in the corridor restrooms beyond the Viennese Room. Three busboys with fire extinguishers created a momentary route to safety across the corridor into the Empire Room. They reached the kitchen just before the Empire Room was completely engulfed in flames. From the kitchen, they escaped through the rear.

The smoke and fire in the North-South Corridor quickly reached the rear doors of the Cabaret Room, sealing off that exit. The doors at the back of the Cabaret Room were, of course, wide open. Heavy black smoke rolled through those doors. There were only two exits left for those in the Cabaret Room, and time was running out.

Meanwhile, the fire and smoke from the North-South Corridor had penetrated the Garden Room. People still in the corridor desperately rushed out via the Garden Room, but the last few people were burned badly. The last group exiting from the kitchen through the Garden Room had to crawl under the smoke to safety.

The Garden Room was empty. Black smoke rolled out the exits. Then the flames erupted through those exits with great force. The windows shattered. Miraculously, everyone exiting through the Garden Room had escaped alive.

Employees in the Cabaret Room yelled at people to remain calm. People in the back yelled for those in front to hurry, and some pushed a little. Long lines extended from both doorways well into the room. Chairs and tables obstructed the floor. People had to move across different levels with metal railings between levels.

Two exits from the Cabaret Room remained and neither led directly to the outside. From the exit on the right, you first had to make an immediate 90 degree left turn, then you had to advance about 20 feet, take a 90 degree right turn and proceed out through a single exterior door above a short, narrow flight of steps. If you made a wrong turn at the start or if you failed to turn and exit at the exterior door, you wound up in a hallway or room with no exterior exit—both were dead ends. From the exit on the left, you had to make an immediate 90 degree left turn, go about 25 feet through a service bar and then out through a set of double doors at ground level. If you went straight instead of turning left, you ended up behind a counter in the service bar. As vision became difficult due to dense smoke, these turns created havoc.

Fire from the North-South Corridor followed the waves of smoke that preceded it into the Cabaret Room. Flames shot through the rear doors 15 to 20 feet into the room. To those in the Cabaret Room, it seemed as if the whole room was exploding into flames.

The descriptions of people who lived through the fiery holocaust give an idea of what it was like:

There were a lot of elderly people in our group. We had helped them as much as we could. But when we saw the fire coming we went over the rail. At that time it was a matter of fighting for your own life. We had been trying to save the people in our tour but it got down to dog eat dog. Save your own life. (Lawson, 1984, p. 184)

I knew I couldn't make it to the door if I got at the end of the line. So I climbed over a rail and jumped from booth to booth until I reached the door. I don't know how but I managed to squeeze into the crowd and got out of the door. As I came through the first door people were starting to fall down. I helped a couple of them to their feet but I was scared. I still don't know how much farther it was to the outside. So I decided to look out for myself. (Lawson, 1984, p. 185)

I screamed at her to get up on the tables. We did that and ran across the tables on the second level toward the service bar and jumped into the crowd. And we were fighting these people to get through, and the smoke had just about covered our heads when we got to the door. (Lawson, 1984, p. 186)

It was just a big mob of people pushing toward the outside. You had no choice but to push along with them. And you had to fight just to stay in line. Otherwise you would have been ground up against the wall somewhere. (Lawson, 1984, pp. 186–187)

Some employees tried to calm people and keep them in lines, but order had broken down. It seemed as if everyone was pushing, and people had to push as hard as everyone else just to maintain their positions and avoid being knocked down. The two small exits were not adequate for the large number of people remaining.

The exit door on the right side of the Cabaret Room opened onto an east-west hallway that ran from the North-South Corridor past the outside single door to a bathroom and the backstage dressing rooms. A door closed this hallway off from the North-South Corridor, protecting it for a while from the smoke and fire, but eventually the smoke in the hallway became overwhelming. Pressing closely against one another, gasping for breath, people pushed out of the Cabaret Room into the hallway, down it to the exit door, and then out, stumbling or falling down the narrow stairs to the grass below. Then the smoke became so dense that once outside the Cabaret Room, people could no longer clearly see the location of the exit. What had been a continuous tightly grouped flow of people became a disconnected, disoriented line. Outside the Cabaret Room, some turned right and headed away from the exit toward the fire. Others turned left but overshot the exterior exit and wound up in the area of the backstage dressing rooms, from which there was no exterior exit. Suddenly flames penetrated the hallway door and engulfed the hallway. With nobody there to hold the outside exit door open, it closed automatically. At the time, there were about 50 people lost somewhere along the hallway or in the backstage dressing rooms. Fire and smoke had cut them off from the outside exit.

By then, firefighters and police had arrived in force. A policeman opened the door from the outside, and a few seconds later a man, black from the smoke, staggered out. No one else came. The policeman crawled one body length into the hallway, but encountered nobody. The smoke caused him to leave. Two firefighters then entered, but the smoke forced them to retreat, gasping for breath.

Firefighters with oxygen tanks arrived and were able to enter. They encountered a pile of people in the hallway outside the Cabaret Room doors. Some were still alive. As quickly as possible, they pulled and carried people outside. They found a man trapped in the service bar directly across the hallway from the exit doors of the Cabaret Room, and they rescued him.

An assistant fire chief, without an air tank, entered and crawled on his hands and knees to his right toward the backstage dressing rooms. He found four or five dead bodies, covered with black soot in the hallway. In the dressing rooms, he found more dead, a few members of the band and a pile of about 15 customers, probably people who had overshot the exit door in the dark. He crawled back out and got help to evacuate the dead. The rescue effort here ended when the fire totally consumed the hallway.

At the left exit from the Cabaret Room in the service bar, two employees, a bartender and a waiter, directed the flow of people toward the outside doors; but dense smoke entered the service bar though the door to the Cabaret Room and through air vents in the ceiling. The bartender, closer to the outside, decided it was time to leave. After he yelled to the waiter, "Let's get the hell out of here!" he exited (Lawson, 1984, p. 193). With the service bar in total darkness and nobody to turn them toward the left, people went straight ahead and became lost behind the counter in the service bar.

Then, horribly, the doorway between the Cabaret Room and the service bar became blocked. A woman was knocked to the floor in the doorway and got stuck with one limb behind the door and the front of her body in the doorway. One after another, those behind her tripped or were pushed. People were piled on top of one another, completely blocking the exit.

Those still inside the Cabaret Room dropped to the floor in hope of getting some oxygen. The smoke was overpowering, and the fire was everywhere. Those caught in the pile tried to extricate themselves, but most were pinned helplessly. For those closest to the floor, there was some oxygen and some protection from the burning heat by the bodies on top of them. Some screamed for help. Others quietly hoped against hope that rescue would come.

Fortunately for those still alive inside, help did come. The bartender who had exited after yelling to his fellow worker found, once outside, that his friend had not followed him. He, along with other employees, reentered. Despite the intense heat, dense smoke, and toxic air, they found several people crawling in the service bar, lost, and pulled them to safety outside.

An off-duty captain from the Cincinnati Fire Department, Peter Sabino, happened to be in the building that night. He had been in the North-South Corridor when word of the fire reached there and had exited out the back through the Garden Room. Later he had reentered with a busboy to see if he could help extinguish the fire in the Zebra Room. By then the fire had spread, and he escaped again, along with the accompanying busboy, via the North-South Corridor and the Garden Room. This time, however, he and the busboy were forced to crawl at top speed down the corridor just ahead of the advancing fire. From outside the Garden Room, he could see people being pulled to safety through the service bar exit doors. He rushed to help. Dropping to his knees at the exit doors, he crawled directly toward the cries of people piled in the doorway at the rear of the service bar. Sabino described what he encountered:

There was just a wall of arms and heads, people piled up at the double doors screaming and waving their arms. I called out for a couple of the employees to give me a hand and I started pulling people, reaching for heads and arms, coats, or anything. They were piled four or five feet high all the way across the doorway. It was just a nightmare. (Lawson, 1984, p. 209)

Sabino had to stop, temporarily overcome by smoke. Beverly Hills personnel, however, including Scott Schilling, the youngest son, and Dick Schilling's brother-in-law, joined the rescue effort. They crawled in and pulled people to safety despite the intense heat and the dense smoke, by then only about 1½ feet from the floor. No human could stay alive for long inside. All those pulled to safety were suffering badly from burns and/or smoke inhalation. The physicians who had been at the Viennese Room party provided immediate first aid here and elsewhere until ambulances arrived.

Firefighters from Southgate and other departments joined the rescue effort. The service bar was cleared completely of the living and the dead. The intensity of the fire in the Cabaret Room precluded entrance from the service bar into that room. It was close to 11:00 P.M.

About the same time, two firefighters battered a hole through the brick wall behind the Cabaret Room stage and found one person still alive, but barely. They pulled the person outside, but that person soon died.

A large number of fire departments from northern Kentucky had arrived quickly, but they had been unable to contain the fire. The firefighters had put great effort into rescuing the living and removing the dead. Now the roof and walls seemed ready to collapse at any moment, and firefighters were still inside. Only dead bodies were being found, and remaining in the building represented a high risk. Sometime close to midnight, the Southgate fire chief ordered that the building be abandoned.

The fire finally burned itself out. The Beverly Hills Supper Club was no more. About 8:00 A.M., the search for additional dead began. The collapsed roof was removed. One of the exterior walls was knocked down. Inside the Cabaret Room beyond the left exit to the service bar, in the debris, the firefighters found 26 bodies (see black areas on Figure 11). They carefully scoured the wreckage of most of the first floor, but no further bodies were found. Evening darkness stopped the search. All the dead had been located except for the two women who had reentered the building and died of smoke inhalation on the second floor.

In the fire, 165 people had died. All but two of those died while trying unsuccessfully to exit the Cabaret Room (see Figure 11). About 58 percent of the dead were women. Only about 20 percent of the dead had been severely burned. The major causes of death were smoke inhalation and carbon monoxide poisoning. About 70 others had been seriously injured. John Davidson, Cabaret Room singer, escaped unharmed.

This was a tragedy of great magnitude. The governor of Kentucky, Julian Carroll, had the commissioner of the state police head an investigation of the fire. The investigative team issued a report on September 16, 1977, identifying electricity as the likely cause of the fire, but the team could not determine either the exact nature of the problem or the exact point of ignition in the walls of the Zebra Room. The

Figure 11
Beverly Hills Fatalities

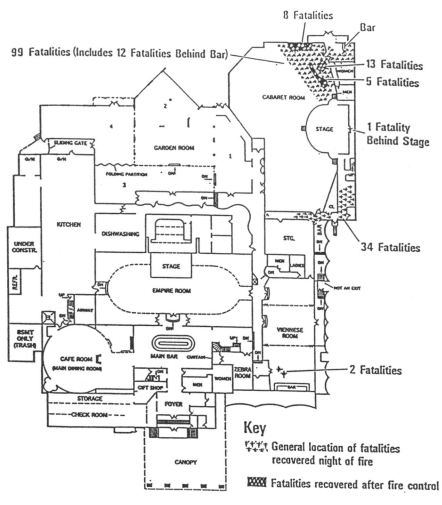

8 Fatalities

Bar

99 Fatalities (Includes 12 Fatalities Behind Bar)

13 Fatalities

5 Fatalities

CABARET ROOM

1 Fatality
Behind Stage

STAGE

34 Fatalities

2 Fatalities

Key

General location of fatalities
recovered night of fire

Fatalities recovered after fire control

REVISED 11/7/77

report identified five main factors causing loss of life:

1. There was delay in spreading the alarm, especially to the Cabaret Room, and slowness in ordering evacuation.
2. There was no evacuation plan and lack of training of personnel in emergency and evacuation procedures.
3. There was gross overcrowding of the Cabaret Room, far beyond the legal occupancy load of the room.
4. In the Cabaret Room, the number and width of exits were inadequate. Furthermore, routes to the outside exits were circuitous and partially obstructed by various impediments, such as railings, service bars, tables, and chairs.
5. The interior finish of the North-South Corridor, especially the paneling and carpeting, did not meet fire-retarding standards. Consequently the fire spread through that hallway to the Cabaret Room with great quickness.

A Campbell County, Kentucky, grand jury was convened to investigate the fire. They were in session through the spring and summer of 1978. On August 2, 1978, a report of the jury's deliberations was released to the public. It contrasted greatly with the report of the investigation team headed by the state police commissioner. The grand jury concluded that the Cabaret Room was not overcrowded, that the exits satisfied the legal requirements, and that there had been no delay in notification of the fire. There had been no criminal negligence. Why had 163 people in the Cabaret Room died? The blame rested mainly with the patrons themselves. The grand jury concluded the following:

It seemed there was a sudden surge of the noxious smoke, hot gases and fire that burst into the Cabaret Room from the main corridor. . . . The result of this occurrence was to create panic among those who had not yet exited the room from the exits which were still available. Testimony also indicated that some patrons of the Cabaret Room, even though notified to evacuate failed to react and remained seated until the conditions of the room itself indicated the need to exit. By this time in some instances it was too late. (Lawson, 1984, p. 271)

Public outcry from survivors, relatives of victims, and the public at large was great. The governor appointed a special prosecutor, Cecil Dunn, to investigate the fire and prepare a recommendation. The report of the special prosecutor was issued in February 1979.

Dunn concluded that the Cabaret Room was definitely overcrowded, exits were inadequate, and there was an eight-to-10 minute delay between discovery of the fire and notification of people in the Cabaret Room. Furthermore, employees were inadequately trained. Although the fire regulations were violated in a number of respects, Dick Schilling, the owner, had, in the end, complied with all demands that inspectors from the state or city had insisted upon. So the blame also rested to some extent on the inspectors who had approved the building.

The special prosecutor concluded that the probability of ultimately convicting Dick Schilling of negligent homicide was remote, given the evidence. Therefore, he recommended against convening a second grand jury to investigate the fire. The governor accepted the recommendation. No one was ever prosecuted for the deaths and injuries suffered in the Beverly Hills fire.

The state fire marshal, the state fire marshal's chief deputy, and the state field inspector for Beverly Hills lost their original jobs. However, the fire marshal continued to work in the office as assistant director in charge of electrical inspections and the other two were moved to a different department. The building inspector of Southgate retained his job.

All legal suits against the owners were settled out of court. All insurance money due the owners and all other assets of the business, principally the land, were given to the claimants in exchange for release from further liability.

Suits against product manufacturers were problematic, since lawyers could not prove which companies had made the materials used at Beverly Hills. In a class action suit, almost 300 claimants sued every manufacturer in industries that made aluminum wiring, wire covering, and materials such as carpets and paneling of the type used at Beverly Hills. The lawyers for the claimants proposed that every manufacturer who might have supplied inadequate materials should be held liable. Included in the suit were Union Light Heat & Power Co., the supplier of power to the club, and Rash-Saville-Crawford, the supplier of the building's air conditioning system. All defendants except one eventually settled out of court; the total payments were estimated to be almost $50 million. The only defendant who refused to settle was Rash-Saville-Crawford, and a jury found that the company was not at fault.

Chapter 7

The Who Concert Stampede, December 3, 1979

Riverfront Coliseum (now called the Crown Coliseum) in Cincinnati, Ohio, opened in September 1975. It is a multi-use indoor arena with over 100 entrance doors placed at various locations around the building.

On the evening of December 3, 1979, the popular British rock band The Who was performing at Riverfront Coliseum. Tickets had gone on sale on September 28, and in just an hour and a half, the concert was sold out. A total of 3,578 tickets were for reserved seats. The remainder of the 18,348 tickets were for festival seating, meaning that a ticket merely entitled the ticket holder to entrance into the building, with seating or standing room in front of the stage determined on a first-come, first-served basis. Consequently, people began to arrive early in the afternoon, long before the doors opened for the 8:00 P.M. performance.

Concern about the use of festival seating at Riverfront Coliseum had been raised several times in the past. A Public Safety Study Team, formed in response to crowd control problems at an Elton John concert in August 1976, reported that the management of Riverfront Coliseum, on its own, was reducing the use of festival seating, and that, therefore, such reductions should be left up to the management. In September 1977, Donald J. Mooney, Jr., of the Cincinnati Human Relations Committee proposed an end to festival seating: "All future concerts should be sold on a reserved seat basis. Reserved seats would discourage the arrival of thousands of fans hours before the concert is scheduled to begin, and before the doors are open. Such congregations, and the resulting drinking and drug abuse, have been the primary causes of disturbances on the plaza level near the coliseum" ('76 Study Recommended Coliseum Reduce "Festival Seating," 1979, p. A–1). The Cincinnati fire division also had raised objections to festival seating, noting that overcrowding and the blockage of aisles tended to occur with festival seating. However, Safety Director Richard Castelleni maintained in a letter to a private citizen that crowd control problems at Riverfront Coliseum were, and should be, the responsibility of management, not the city: "enforcement of codes and ordinances would and could be handled by coliseum personnel, as enforcement was above and beyond the capabilities of the limited manpower of the fire division and exceeds the service to which a privately owned facility is entitled" (Delaney & Greenfield, 1979, p. B–1).

By 7:00 P.M., thousands were tightly packed around the entrance doors (see Figure 12), creating a dangerous situation, as the following account by a 17-year-old girl indicates:

I lost my footing an' slowly but surely began going down. People behind me could do nothing to stop the pushing. I was saying "No. No. Please help me . . ." Some of the people around didn't even hear me. . . . So then I grabbed someone's leg an' whoever that was told three other guys about me. They all pushed me up, pulled me up, but it was hard. . . . At about 7 o'clock I passed out. The four guys who pulled me off the ground helped me to stay up until we got through the door. (Johnson, 1987, p. 367)

Police Lieutenant Dale Menkhaus headed a squad of 25 Cincinnati police whose responsibility was crowd control outside the arena. Menkhaus met with off-duty Police Sergeant John Basham, the coordinator of private security inside the coliseum, and Cal Levy, the local promoter for Electric Factory Concerts. Menkhaus urged that the doors be opened, but Levy balked. The Who were late in arriving and needed time for a sound check. Furthermore, only a small number of ticket takers had arrived. The doors remained closed.

By 7:20 P.M., the crowd outside numbered about 8,000, according to the estimate of a police officer on the scene. People edged ever closer to the locked entrance doors. The densely packed crowd began to sway back and forth, as people deliberately tried to create a "wave." From time to time, someone at the fringe of the crowd would shove forward trying to create a new "wave."

The crowd became even more tightly bunched. One person stated afterward that the crush was so great he could not lift his arm in order to scratch his head. Still, one person commented to the person next to him, "If you think this is bad, you should have been at the Led Zeppelin concert; this is nothing" (Johnson, 1987, p. 370). A security guard later expressed a similar view of the crowd congestion, "We always have that . . . . We have handled a lot of shows, concerts, and I thought some of them were worse than this one" (Johnson, 1987, p. 370).

Just after 7:20 P.M., a side door was opened (see E on Figure 12). The police believed that the door was forced open from the outside by gate crashers, but a 27-year-old male ticket holder maintained afterward that the door was opened by two men inside to prevent injury to "two young girls [who] had been banging on the door for 20 minutes" (Johnson, 1987, p. 370). The police secured the door.

About 7:30 P.M., the north and south banks of doors outside the lobby were finally opened (see A and B on Figure 12). Each bank of doors contained eight doors, but according to many in the crowd, not all these doors were opened. The crowd surged forward, and people closest to the doors felt extraordinary pressure from behind. The density was so great that some people were lifted off the concrete surface and carried forward, unable for a time to get their feet back on the ground. A number of people lost their shoes.

Figure 12
Riverfront Coliseum

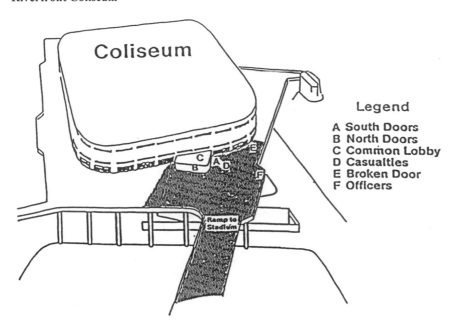

Coliseum

Legend

A South Doors
B North Doors
C Common Lobby
D Casualties
E Broken Door
F Officers

Ramp to Stadium

• *Diagram of Cincinnati's Riverfront Coliseum and Surrounding Plaza, Site of "The Who Concert Stampede," with Area of Densest Occupancy Shaded and Referenced Locations Marked*

Norris Johnson, "The Who Concert Stampede." Reprinted by permission from *Social Problems*, vol. 34, no. 4, p. 366. © 1987 by The Society for the Study of Social Problems.

When the lobby was full, the guards would temporarily close most of the north and south doors until there was room for more. Whenever the guards closed the outer doors, some people became concerned that the arena was already full. Furthermore, the clearly audible sounds of the band warming up may have added to the sense of urgency.

Then at an area outside the south doors, some people fell (see D on Figure 12). The people behind those who had fallen were pushed forward by the inexorable force of the crowd. Those on the ground were being trampled. Some tried to pull them up, but it was not possible to hold back the crowd. Others tripped and fell on top of those who were down. A pile of about 25 people resulted, sometimes three to five people deep.

Some people caught in the situation attributed the actions of others to a lack of knowledge and to the pressure of the crowd, as the following accounts indicate:

At that point everyone around the perimeter of the circle, of course, was trying to back off and trying to help the people get up onto their feet, but the people in the back of the crowd, of course, could not see this and continued to push forward. (Johnson, 1987, p. 368)

People in the crowd 10 feet back didn't know it was happening. Their cries were impossible to hear above the roar of the crowd. . . . I screamed with all my strength that I was standing on someone. I couldn't move. I could only scream. (Johnson, 1987, p. 368)

There was really no way they could help me because there were so many people tryin' ta shove over the top of me that they would have to clear all them out just even to see me. (Johnson, 1987, p. 369)

On the other hand, some people attributed the actions of others to a lack of concern and to the desire to procure a good place or seat, as the following accounts indicate:

They just kept pushin' forward and they would just walk right on top of you, just trample over ya like you were a piece of the ground. They wouldn't even help ya; people were just screamin' "help me" and nobody cared. (Johnson, 1987, p. 368)

I knew she was unconscious or something. And then everybody just trampled her like she wasn't even there; they just standin' on her. (Johnson, 1987, p. 368)

And there was this big group of people in front of me that had fallen down and people just went mad. They kept, you know, shovin' over me; they wouldn't help them get up; they wanted inside . . . . I fell down with them and no one helped me up and I—there was no way I could get up—and they just kept—there was people fallin' on me and then people walkin' over my legs tryin' ta get through the door. (Johnson, 1987, p. 369)

Initially, the police and the security guards were unaware of the dangerous situation outside the south doors, because the density of the crowd prohibited police and security guards from circulating. The security guards were primarily concerned with regulating the flow of the crowd through the exterior doors (see A and B on

Figure 12) into the lobby (see C on Figure 12) and making sure that no one could sneak past the turnstiles that separated the outer lobby from the interior.

Some of the crowd, aware of the threatening nature of the situation, tried to convince Coliseum personnel that more doors should be opened, but without success, as the following account attests:

[He] tried to shove open some more doors with his foot and immediately two ushers came up, one of them grabbed him, shoved him back in line and told him to either get in line or get back out. He then began to beg and plead with the usher, he said, "people are getting hurt, people were down." (Johnson, 1987, p. 370)

Finally, police officers on the fringe of the crowd (at F on Figure 12) noticed that someone was on the ground, though they did not grasp initially the full nature of the situation. At 7:54 P.M., an officer radioed, "Emergency . . . we need a life squad. Coliseum on the concourse level. We have a man down, a possible heart attack" (Johnson, 1987, p. 365).

The police worked their way through the crowd as fast as they could, but given the extraordinary density, that was a difficult task. Finally they reached the pile, but for some it was too late. Eleven people were trampled to death, dying of asphyxiation, and others required hospitalization. The dead, seven males and four females, ranged in age from 15 to 22.

J. Kenneth Blackwell, just installed as mayor on December 1, was informed of the deaths, and he conferred with other city officials, including Safety Director Richard Castelleni, whose son was at the concert. They decided to let the concert continue. The Who and most of the audience were unaware of the deaths until later.

As a result of The Who Concert tragedy, Cincinnati formed the Task Force of Crowd Control and Safety. At the recommendation of this task force, an ordinance was passed making festival seating illegal for indoor events with over 2,000 patrons.

Counterpoint:
Case Histories of Successes

By way of contrast, we have selected two historical examples of very successful exiting. The first involves exiting from a crashed plane under severe time pressure. The second is a case where following an explosion, tens of thousands evacuated several high-rise office buildings, including two of the tallest buildings in the world. In both cases, the coordination of traffic flow was extraordinary.

Chapter 8

Trans World Airlines Jet Crash, July 30, 1992

On July 30, 1992, at 1716 (5:16 P.M.), Trans World Airlines (TWA) flight 843 from New York to San Francisco received clearance to leave its loading gate at John F. Kennedy International Airport (JFK). The plane was a wide-body Lockheed L1011.

The flight had a crew of 12: Captain William Kinkead, First Officer Dennis Hergert, Second Officer (flight engineer) Charles Long, and nine flight attendants. There were 280 passengers, including two off-duty pilots, both seated in cockpit jumpseats, and five off-duty flight attendants, three seated in extra cabin attendant positions and two seated in passenger seats. Every seat on the plane was occupied.

As directed by ground control, the plane taxied to runway 13R/31L, the longest runway, 14,572 feet in length, at JFK. At 1740, the plane was cleared for takeoff.

First Officer Dennis Hergert was at the controls. At TWA, it was standard operating procedure when the first officer is at the controls during takeoff for the captain to control the thrust levers until the landing gear is retracted. Captain Kinkead advanced the power for takeoff, and the plane accelerated normally. At 1741:09.4, flight 843 lifted off the runway.

As the plane became airborne, the first officer and the captain felt their control columns shake. The plane had two independent Angle of Attack (AOA) sensors, one on each side of the fuselage. These sensors detect when the plane's AOA, given the flap/slat configuration, is approaching the value at which a stall will occur. This stickshaker warning mechanism caused the captain's and first officer's control columns to vibrate. Although the control columns were shaking, indicating that a stall was imminent, in reality the engines were functioning normally and there was no danger of a stall. A mechanical malfunction in the right AOA sensor had sent a false warning.

The first officer, in reaction to his vibrating control column, either pushed or allowed the control column to move forward, thereby diminishing the rate of acceleration somewhat. At 1741:11.4, the first officer said, "Gettin a stall" (National Transportation Safety Board, 1993, p. 3). At 1741:12.8, the first officer said,

"You got it," and yielded control of the airplane to the captain (National Transportation Safety Board, 1993, p. 3). At 1741:13.7, the captain replied, "OK" (National Transportation Safety Board, 1993, p. 3).

Captain Kinkead was faced with a split second decision. Standard procedure called for the pilot to complete the takeoff and then return for a landing. However, taking into consideration the stall warning, his own perception that the plane was sinking and would not fly, and the fact that a considerable length of runway was still ahead, the captain decided to abort.

Captain Kinkead closed the thrust levers and put the L1011 back on the runway. The wheels touched down at 1741:15.4. The plane had been airborne for exactly six seconds. The captain used full reverse thrust and maximum breaking in an effort to stop the plane before the end of the runway.

At 1741:35.3, a fire warning bell sounded inside the plane. At 1741:38.2, the control tower at JFK informed the crew, "TWA eight forty three heavy, numerous flames" (National Transportation Safety Board, 1993, p. 3).

The plane was above maximum landing weight, since almost no fuel had been consumed, the descent, about 14 feet per second, was more rapid than the structural limit, and the right wing was slightly low at landing. As a result, when the right main landing gear touched down, the force exceeded the structural design limit, causing fractures in the right wing rear spar. Fuel escaped and ignited. The fuselage from the wing back, especially on the right side, and the tail were aflame.

To Captain Kinkead, it was now apparent that while the plane was slowing, it would not stop in time to avoid a collision with the blast fence at the end of the runway. Consequently, he turned the plane left, directing it off the runway toward an open area. As the plane left the runway, the nose wheel collapsed. Flight 843 finally stopped in the grass adjacent to runway 13R/31L.

Extinguisher agent bottles were activated by the crew. Just after the fuel and ignition switches were turned off by the captain, the evacuation alarm sounded. The captain spoke to the passengers and crew over the public address system, "This is the captain, evacuate the aircraft" (National Transportation Safety Board, 1993, p. 5). Then he entered the cabin in order to assist with the evacuation.

There were 14 flight attendants on board, nine on duty and five off duty. All 14 went into action, directing the evacuation. The L1011 had eight exit doors, four on each side. Only exits L-1, L-2, and R-1 were used. On the right side, the R-3 and R-4 doors were not opened due to fire immediately outside. At R-3, fingers of flames invaded the cabin. Flight attendants then blocked that exit, directing people toward the usable exits. Door R-1 was opened, and the emergency chute deployed. Doors L-3, L-4, and R-2 were opened, but there was fire and smoke immediately outside. Flight attendants blocked those doors and sent the passengers forward. At first, the attendant at L-2 was reluctant to open that emergency exit door, because she could not see clearly through the cloudy glass. She stationed an off-duty attendant at L-2 and moved to another window. From that window, she could see that the L-2 exit was free of flames. She signaled for the L-2 exit to be opened. Door L-1 on the left side was opened also. The emergency chutes for those two doors popped out.

Although some were initially unaware of the fire, the degree of danger was soon readily apparent to all. According to Lewelyn DeGuzman, a 45-year-old woman from California: "I could see death. I could see flames" (Myers, 1992, p. B2).

William Kistner, a retired police officer from California, described his reactions: "When they opened the doors, the smoke started pouring into the plane. People were coughing. Suddenly it was very hard to breathe. I thought, 'We have a full tank of gas, there's fire, it's time to get off the airplane' " (McFadden, 1992, p. B2).

Julia Elhauge, a 31-year-old woman from California, expressed her fears: "If I was killed, it would be excruciatingly painful. I thought this will hurt, so I need to move out of here quickly" (Myers, 1992, p. B2).

The passengers moved quickly. In perhaps two minutes, certainly within three minutes, all 292 people aboard had exited safely. The captain, after checking that everyone else had exited, was the last to leave.

All the flight attendants, including the ones who were off duty, performed admirably. Passenger Lewelyn DeGuzman described her experience with the flight attendant who guided her and her daughter to safety: "She was very helpful. She told us not to panic. Just go all the way. You could see flames and fire. 'Don't panic,' she said, 'or don't shout or we won't get out' " (Treaster, 1992, p. B2).

Tara Brock, an officer for the Association of Flight Attendants, explained that training involved simulations of "airplanes crashing, noise and smoke and the tilting of the airplane, fire, smoke, and darkness . . . . That's really what we're trained to do. Evacuate airplanes upside down, in the dark and in the water (Treaster, 1992, p. B2).

According to *The New York Times* article of July 31, 1992, by Robert D. McFadden, "Passengers told of almost no panic, little screaming or pushing—an almost eerie sense of order amid the glow of flames and the life-or-death evacuation—and aviation authorities later said a disaster that might have cost hundreds of lives had been averted" (McFadden, 1992, p. A1).

Firefighters arrived at the crash site within three minutes. All on board had exited by then. The fuselage, the tail, and the inside of the rear cabin were ablaze. The fire was virtually extinguished in about five to six minutes, but it continued to smolder for about 40 minutes after the crash, when it was completely extinguished. The plane was a total loss, the fire having seriously damaged most of the plane from the wings back. The injuries incurred while exiting were relatively minor. The most serious was a broken leg.

This true account of exiting efficiency seems astounding. To accomplish the rate of exiting achieved, 292 people in 120 to 180 seconds, the people aboard needed to exit with an extremely high level of coordination, without either blockage caused by too many people trying to exit at the same time or delays caused by the hesitation of some people in exiting. While it may seem unlikely that another set of 292 people could duplicate that level of exiting coordination, we will argue in the last chapter that achieving such coordination is well within the capacity of almost any set of 292 airplane evacuees provided that certain requirements are met.

Chapter 9

World Trade Center Bombing, February 26, 1993

At about 8:00 on the morning of Friday, February 26, 1993, school buses loaded with children from five kindergarten classes departed from Public School (P.S.) 95 in the Gravesend section of Brooklyn. It was the annual field trip to the World Trade Center. Three of the classes would be back by midafternoon, as scheduled; but for two of the classes, the field trip would take much longer than expected.

The World Trade Center is actually a complex of seven high-rise buildings in lower Manhattan (see Figure 13), but for most people, the World Trade Center is synonymous with the Twin Towers, each with 110 stories, and a quarter-mile high. Each of the Twin Towers is among the tallest buildings in the world.

One of the seven buildings is separated from the others by Vesey Street (see Figure 13). The other six buildings are built over an underground area containing a shopping mall, four levels of parking, and a major station for the Port Authority Trans-Hudson (PATH) commuter trains.

The World Trade Center is huge. It has seven times the office space of the Empire State Building. About 50,000 people work at the World Trade Center, and it is estimated that about 80,000 others will come there at one time or another during a typical day.

On the 107th floor of Tower Two is an observatory that provides a spectacular view. The kindergarten classes from P.S. 95 in Brooklyn would be visiting the observatory that day.

At 12:18 P.M., an explosion ripped through six underground parking levels beneath the Vista Hotel at a position adjacent to Tower One. The blast was caused by a 1,500-pound bomb placed in a van, and was the work of a group of terrorists. The van was parked in the second sublevel, the B-2 level, of the underground garage (see Figure 14). The explosion produced a gigantic crater about 200 feet wide. The blast penetrated upward into the lobby of the Vista Hotel and shattered the glass partitions between the Vista Hotel and Tower One. Masonry fire walls and fire doors between the Vista Hotel and Tower One were demolished. The blast pene-

Figure 13
World Trade Center Complex

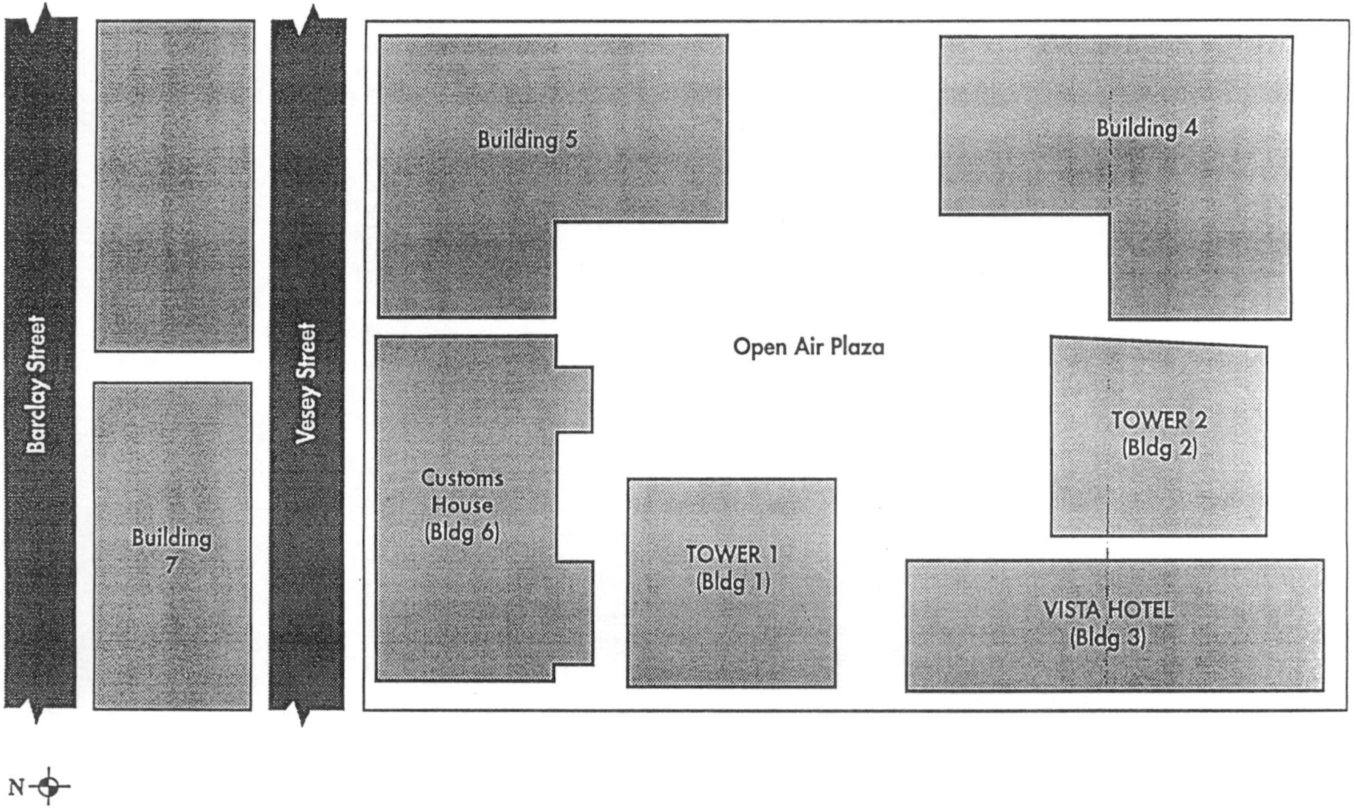

Reprinted with permission from *NFPA Journal*®, National Fire Protection Association, Quincy, MA 02269. *NFPA Journal*® is a registered trademark of the National Fire Protection Association, Inc.

92

Figure 14
World Trade Center Explosion

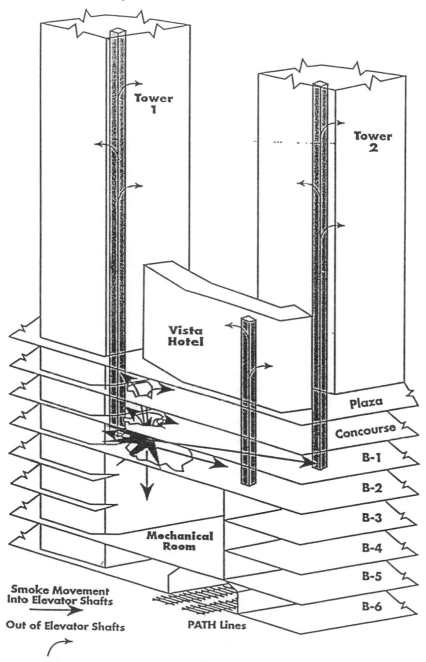

Tower 1

Tower 2

Vista Hotel

Plaza

Concourse

B-1

B-2

B-3

B-4

B-5

B-6

Mechanical Room

Smoke Movement Into Elevator Shafts

Out of Elevator Shafts

PATH Lines

trated downward through the floor of the B-2 level, causing the floor slabs of that level and the levels above to fall through open space onto electrical, communication, and water systems equipment at levels B-5 and B-6.

Six people who were in close proximity to the explosion were killed. Five were men, and the sixth was a woman, in her seventh month of pregnancy. The fetus was killed also. Five died instantly. The sixth was rushed to a hospital, but he died at 2:20 P.M. of smoke inhalation and traumatic cardiac arrest.

Fires erupted in the immediate area of the blast. Thick, oily smoke filled the lobby areas of the Vista Hotel and Tower One and entered the elevator shafts of both buildings. Underground, smoke spread through the basement area, entering additional elevator shafts of Tower One and the elevator shafts of Tower Two and Four World Trade Center, a nine-story office building containing the New York headquarters for commodity trading (see Building 4 on Figure 13). The smoke rose rapidly into the upper levels of the buildings. The Vista Hotel and Tower One were most affected, Tower Two a little less so, and Four World Trade Center was affected only slightly.

The blast severely damaged the main power source, leaving only three of the eight primary power feeds operating. The fire department ordered the remaining feeds shut down until the fires were extinguished. An emergency generator kicked on, but it soon shut down, because the blast had severed the pipes that carried water to cool its engines. Without any electricity, the hallways and stairwells were in darkness. Furthermore, the absence of electricity meant that smoke could not be drawn out of the stairwells by reversing the fans.

The operations control center was severely damaged. Internal telephones, closed-circuit television monitors, and the public address system were inoperative in the Twin Towers and the Commodities Exchange. With all interior communication systems gone, the evacuation plan for the Twin Towers could not be implemented.

An evacuation plan was part of fire security at the World Trade Center. Although the state legislature declared the World Trade Center exempt from New York City's stringent high-rise fire code, the Center followed most of the code, including the requirement for fire safety teams on each floor. Each tenant was required to assign people to the fire safety team. The team received training from a World Trade Center fire safety director, and that training included sections on the location of exits and stairways and on the evacuation plan. In case of a fire in one of the Twin Towers, the two stairways farthest away from the fire should be used, so that the third stairway, the one closest to the fire, would be free for use by the fire department. Five floors would be evacuated at a time, starting with the fire floor, the floor above and the three floors below. In order to implement the plan, members of the fire safety team had to be told which stairways to use and which floors to evacuate at a particular time. The destruction of the operations center severed communication systems to the fire safety teams, so the evacuation plan could not be implemented.

Although drills were held twice a year, the preparedness of fire safety teams was something of a sham. Questionnaire research conducted afterward by the National Fire Protection Association revealed that during the drills in the Twin Towers, the vast majority of fire safety team members never left their own floors, much less the building (Fahy & Proulx, 1995). Many members of fire safety teams in the Twin Towers did not know where all three stairways were located. It is not surprising, then, that the safety teams played little, if any, role during the evacuation. For the most part, people were left to fend for themselves.

Most outside phone lines from tenants' offices were still operative. The first emergency 911 call reporting the explosion was made within four seconds. Firefighters, police, and emergency medical personnel arrived quickly and immediately began rescue and fire-fighting operations. Before the day was out, about 45 percent of the on-duty resources of the New York City Fire Department would be in action, the largest single response in the history of that department.

People in the Twin Towers were aware that something terrible had happened, but they did not know what. Denise Bosco, a secretary who worked on the 82nd floor for the Port Authority of New York and New Jersey, described her reactions:

The whole building shook. The lights flashed on and off. The computers went down. Then, instantly, there was smoke. I was terrified. People panicked. They started pushing and shouting to get out. Some of them were throwing up. I said, "Oh dear God, what is it? What is it? Is it my time? Is this the way?" It was horrible. There was this awful feeling that we might not be able to get out. We were in the mighty, tall tower but we weren't getting out. (Kleinfield, 1993, p. 1)

The firefighters set out to evacuate all seven buildings of the World Trade Center, but top priority was given to the evacuation of the Vista Hotel, which was immediately above the explosion. The Vista Hotel has 825 rooms and is 22 stories high. Unlike the Twin Towers and the Commodities Exchange, the fire alarm and voice communication systems were still operational in the Vista Hotel. These systems were used to coordinate the evacuation. The building was evacuated by all occupants in about 15 minutes. The firefighters searched every room to ensure no one was overlooked, and that search was completed in about an hour. Then primary attention was directed toward the evacuation of the Twin Towers.

Meanwhile, the other buildings were being evacuated without difficulty. The Commodities Exchange received only a relatively small amount of smoke, so although its communication systems were down, evacuation was not problematical. Buildings 5, 6, and 7 were not affected by the explosion except for the initial tremor.

When the bomb exploded, the five kindergarten classes from P.S. 95 were scattered. One of the classes was already on the bus, ready for the return trip to Brooklyn. Two others were in the lobby of Tower Two, about to leave. The two classes in the lobby were dispersed by the large crowd exiting there, but teachers and helpers guided all of the children outside to the buses. One class was on an elevator, and one was in the cafeteria on floor 107 of Tower Two.

With all electricity gone, elevators stopped where they were, sometimes between floors. Ann Marie Tesoriero's P.S. 95 kindergarten class was in a crowded elevator on the way down to ground level following their visit to the observatory on the 107th floor of Tower Two. Suddenly the lights inside the elevator flickered, then went out, and the elevator stopped—between floors 35 and 36. They were stuck.

The smell of smoke became evident. Tesoriero urged the 17 children not to worry. She had them sing songs. She pulled out a rosary that glowed in the dark and led those who wished to join her in reciting Hail Marys. Their wait was just beginning. It would be five hours before help would come.

Because the explosion occurred at 12:18 P.M., many people were at lunch, either at a restaurant in another building or at a fast food restaurant on the first floor. Those on the lower floors, including those at the fast food places, exited quickly and without much difficulty, although there was some pushing and shoving. As smoke grew thicker in the stairwells and hallways, those on the upper floors were confronted with a difficult decision: go up to the roof, stay in the office, or walk down through the smoke.

A few went up to the Tower Two roof. Police helicopters evacuated over 30 people from there.

Many stayed put. Fire experts often favor this option when stairwells and hallways contain thick smoke. All doors to the hallway should be closed and material should be jammed around the edges. Air vents should be closed and blocked by stuffing material into them. If there is no smoke outside and the smoke inside has become thick, windows should be opened manually. Generally, experts advise against breaking windows, because often smoke will rise up along the outside of the building and enter through broken windows, which cannot be closed again. Furthermore, falling glass could endanger people below. At the World Trade Center, some people broke exterior windows. Fortunately, however, the amount of exterior smoke was not great.

Many walked down the black, smoky stairs. The stairwells were dark, but a few people had found flashlights, and others occasionally struck a match in order to see. There were reports of some people crying and a few people screaming as they made the long trek down, but the vast majority remained calm despite the smoke. When people saw a pregnant woman, she was allowed to go on ahead if able to do so. Several people who used wheelchairs were carried down by teams of friends, in one case 37 floors and in another 66 floors. In general, then, people gave support and encouragement to others. Racquel Vidal, a legal assistant, gave the following account of her descent from floor 103:

About the 40th floor, my knees starting to give in. I didn't think I was going to make it. But my co-workers kept egging me on. Let's keep going, they'd say. We only have 40 floors to go. We only have 30. We only have 20. So I kept going, and I'm not sure my knees will ever forgive me. (Kleinfield, 1993, p. 22)

The darkness, the smoke, the crowds, the fatigue, and the uncertainty of what lay ahead all combined to make the hike down a difficult one. Several people described the difficulties of the walk down a tower stairwell:

It was like sardines, cattle, a herd. (McFadden, 1993, p. 22)

You couldn't even see it was so smoky. I kept wanting to sit down but I didn't because if

I sat down I thought I wouldn't get up. (McFadden, 1993, p. 22)

The closer to ground level, the denser the crowds on the stairs of the Twin Towers became. At each floor, additional people might enter, merging with the group already on the stairs; but the flow of people was maintained without disruption.

The fires did not escape the basement level, and the firefighters extinguished the worst of them by midafternoon. Firefighters, medics, and police made their way up the stairways of the Twin Towers, carrying flashlights and emergency oxygen equipment. They provided information, encouragement, temporary relief from the darkness, and emergency medical assistance to the people heading downward.

Rosemarie Russo's kindergarten class from P.S. 95 was in the cafeteria on the 107th floor of Tower Two when the explosion occurred. When smoke billowed into the cafeteria, Russo moved the class outside to the observatory. For three hours they waited outside in the cold and light snow. Finally, several firefighters and police arrived, having walked up the 107 floors. Using flashlights, they escorted the children down. On floor 94, the children stopped for soft drinks and snacks in an office where people were still waiting. Then they continued down. Several hours later, they emerged safely at ground level of Tower Two.

Late in the afternoon, Fire Department Lieutenants Michael Podolak and James Sherwood, using sledgehammers, broke through the wall of the elevator stuck between the 35th and 36th floors of Tower Two. The last of the P.S. 95 classes was saved.

The smoke was particularly bad in some of the elevator shafts. Firefighter Michael Dugan gave the following account of a rescue in Tower One:

We opened an elevator door and found people who had been in there for at least two hours. There were 10 people lying on the floor. None of them was moving. It was like a scene from a movie. All we could hear was one woman crying. The rest were semiconscious with coats thrown over their faces. They were five or 10 minutes from death. (Kleinfield, 1993, p. 22)

At the time of the explosion there may have been as many as 50,000 people in the Twin Towers, yet all but the six killed by the blast itself exited alive. Although many required medical treatment for smoke inhalation, no one died of smoke inhalation due to slowness in exiting. There was some pushing and shoving, particularly by people on the lower levels immediately after the explosion, but no one was injured or killed due to being trampled on by others.

Newsweek writers Tom Mathews, Karen Breslau, Patrick Rogers, and Marc Peyser attributed the successful evacuation to the nature of New Yorkers: "New York pluck, born of blackouts and subway fires, came to the rescue . . . . If the disaster had struck a city less self-possessed than New York, hundreds might have been trampled to death" (Mathews, Breslau, Rogers, & Peyser, 1993, p. 27).

Chapter 10

Conclusions from Case Histories

What caused the extreme physical competition, such as pushing others out of the way, knocking others down, and trampling on others, that eventually occurred in the five cases of dysfunctional traffic flow? We believe that the following 10 factors, occurring in combination, produce these extreme forms of competitive behavior. As we shall see, six of these 10 factors were present in all five case histories of poor traffic flow. The other four factors, while not present in all five cases of dysfunctional traffic flow, contributed to the problem when they were present.

We have divided the 10 factors into three categories: preconditions, reactions to the precipitating events, and factors once the traffic flow is strong. The 10 factors are:

PRECONDITIONS
1. There are severe limitations on the amount of passage space and/or on the number, width, or location of exterior openings.
2. A large number of people are present.
3. There is widespread lack of knowledge about some of the available paths and the location of some of the exterior openings.
4. There is a lack of an adequate emergency plan or the lack of adequate training in the implementation of the plan.

REACTIONS TO THE PRECIPITATING EVENTS
5. There is the widespread perception of serious negative consequences for the failure to exit or enter by some time limit.
6. There is the widespread perception of a severe limitation on the time available to exit or enter.
7. There is a strong response tendency to use the most familiar or most salient path and exterior opening.

8.   There is an inability of potential leaders to exert influence.

FACTORS ONCE THE TRAFFIC FLOW IS STRONG

9.   The crowd density is so great that independence of individual action is lost to a considerable extent.

10. There is a failure to keep the exterior openings clear beyond those openings.
      These factors will be elaborated upon below:

PRECONDITIONS

1.   There are severe limitations on the amount of passage space and/or on the number, width, or location of exterior openings. These limitations can be inherent in the architectural design of the structure or they can be imposed by people on an adequately designed structure.

The design of the building can have aisles, stairs, or halls that are too narrow for the rapid passage of a large crowd. The passageways can be too few in number. There can be steps placed so that tripping over those steps is common during rapid movement. A potential problem that may be ignored in the design of the building concerns the adequacy of space when two separate streams of pedestrians flow into one another. For example, when the stream of people coming down from the balcony meets the stream of people exiting on the first floor, is there adequate space to accommodate all?

The design can have an inadequate number of exterior openings, openings of too small a width, or openings that are not dispersed adequately around the structure. A sufficient number of exterior openings of sufficient width is, of course, necessary if a large crowd is to pass through the openings rapidly. Adequate dispersion is important because dispersion allows for quick passage through the exterior openings by people coming from different locations and because access to one part of the structure can become closed by events such as a fire or explosion.

Structural problems can be exacerbated or a problem can be introduced into an otherwise adequate structure by certain alterations in the environment. Pathways can be obstructed by objects such as furniture. Exterior doors can be locked. The location of stairs, hallways, or doors can be obscured by dim lighting, by inadequate signs, or by the total absence of signs. Doors to hallways or the exterior can be camouflaged by making them appear to be something else, such as the continuation of the wall, or they can be covered by objects or draperies.

2.   A large number of people are present. The number of people attempting to exit or enter is a major factor causing poor traffic flow. In real evacuation circumstances, the more people are present, the greater the ratio of people to hall width or stair width or total exterior door width is. So it is not surprising that large crowds work against efficient flow. Interestingly enough in laboratory experiments, if you give larger groups more time so that the ratio of group size to time available is held constant or if you give larger groups more exit space so that the ratio of group size to exit space is held constant, larger groups still are less efficient at exiting than smaller groups (Chertkoff, Kushigian, & McCool, 1996; Kelley et al., 1965). For example, a six-person group usually will get a lower percentage of the group out than a three-person group if, for groups of both sizes, there is room for only one

person to exit at a time but six-person groups have twice as much time to get everyone out as three-person groups do. Likewise, a six-person group typically will get a lower percentage out than a three-person group if they both have the same amount of time, but a six-person group is given twice as much exit space. Size itself is an enemy of traffic flow efficiency.

3. There is widespread lack of knowledge about some of the available paths and the location of some of the exterior openings. Sometimes people only know of one exterior door and one path. People in a night club or theater for the first time may be totally ignorant of any door or path other than the door and path they used to reach their tables or seats. It is not surprising that visitors to a structure, especially those who have seldom or never been there before, should lack knowledge. However, even people who work at the building can be ignorant concerning some pathways and exterior doors.

If the exterior door a person used initially is distant or the path to it is blocked by people or fire or debris, the person may do a visual search for other paths, ones leading hopefully to other exterior doors. The visual prominence of these alternative paths and doors becomes crucial. If people are unfamiliar with the structure, it is especially important that signs, such as exit signs, be prominent and that pathways and doors not be camouflaged or covered.

4. There is a lack of an adequate emergency plan or the lack of adequate training in the implementation of the plan. A good plan should specify the duties of all staff members and the paths people in various locations should use. A good plan should also anticipate various possibilities and specify what should be done in each situation. For example, if access to the preferred exit is blocked, what should people do?

The absence of a good plan with contingencies for alterations in the situation can be an invitation to disaster. Without such a plan, the spread of an alarm about the danger and the spread of information about the nature and location of the danger is likely to be haphazard. Without such a plan, people are left to make snap decisions about where to go without careful, informed consideration about what is best for the individual or the entire group. Those hurried, uninformed decisions may lead to the overutilization of some paths and the underutilization of others.

A good plan, however, is just a beginning. All people responsible for carrying out the plan need to know the plan very well and their required actions need to be well rehearsed. Factors such as emotional arousal caused by danger, obscured vision caused by smoke, and the soporific state caused by carbon monoxide can affect memory of the plan and one's ability to carry it out effectively. Only if the plan has been so well rehearsed that the responses are automatic, meaning they do not involve conscious deliberation, is the plan likely to be carried out successfully under a grave emergency.

REACTIONS TO THE PRECIPITATING EVENTS

5. There is the widespread perception of serious negative consequences for the failure to exit or enter by some time limit. Until such a perception becomes widespread, people do not shove others out of the way, knock them down, trample on

them. To the contrary, they may even move lethargically or remain where they are.

In evacuating a building, people are likely to use physical force in competition for access to the exit when very serious injury or death are perceived to be the likely outcome for the failure to exit quickly. In entering a structure, people are likely to use physical force in competition for the entrance when the outcome for failure to enter quickly results in, for example, a very poor seat or even no seat at all, missing a significant part of the show, or not obtaining some desirable object.

Laboratory experiments conducted by Kelley and his associates (Kelley et al., 1965) clearly indicate that the greater the penalty for failure to exit by some time limit, the fewer the proportion of people who exit successfully. A larger penalty causes too many to try to exit at once, jamming the exit so that none can exit.

6. There is the widespread perception of a severe limitation on the time available to exit or enter. The perception of a serious negative consequence for the failure to exit or enter is not likely to lead to the use of physical force unless it is accompanied by the perception that there is very little time available. These two factors in combination cause a strong desire to move quickly.

In a laboratory experiment, Chertkoff et al. (1996) found that the less time available, the poorer the coordination of exiting. Even when the consequences for failure to exit are minor, a short time limit on exiting causes too many to try to exit at once.

A questionnaire study of people at the Beverly Hills Supper Club Fire indicated that a physical struggle for access to the exits only occurred in the Cabaret Room once intense fire and smoke invaded the room (Johnson, 1988). Before it became clear that death was imminent unless one escaped very quickly, exiting was orderly, at the start perhaps even sluggish, with nothing worse than a slight push designed to speed up those in front. Likewise, a questionnaire study of people at The Who Concert suggested that the sound of the band playing (actually they were only warming up) led many to think that the concert was already underway and that they would miss a significant part of it (Johnson, 1987).

7. There is a strong response tendency to use the most familiar or most salient path and exterior opening. This tendency is well documented in questionnaire studies of people involved in actual emergency evacuations (e.g., Sime, 1985). Even when people are knowledgeable about alternative paths and exits, they tend to use the most familiar or most salient path.

This tendency can be explained psychologically as being due to the effects of increased arousal on cognitive functioning and on behavioral choices. Judgment and decision-making research undertaken in the field of psychology clearly shows that increased arousal, such as would be produced by situations involving emergency exiting, causes people to attend to a narrower range of aspects of the situation and to consider a narrower range of options (Janis & Mann, 1977). In the extreme, we may attend to and consider only one possible way out. Furthermore, high emotional arousal causes us to favor even more strongly our dominant response tendencies (Zajonc, 1965). If one path out of a building is the one we use most often, though not always, increased arousal will increase the probability of using the favorite path.

8. There is an inability of potential leaders to exert influence. An inability of potential leaders to effect an orderly flow of people can stem from a wide number of factors, including the failure of potential leaders to assume the leadership position, the inability of the leaders to communicate, ineffective communication, or the reluctance of the audience to heed the directives of the person trying to influence them.

Potential leaders may not engage in leadership acts because it is not clear who should assume leadership. A good plan should specify who should occupy the leadership roles and what the responsibility of each leader is. Even in the absence of a formal plan, it may be obvious due to an existing hierarchy who should act as leader. Research by Johnston and Johnson (1988) indicates that workers, such as waiters or waitresses, who serve patrons directly often provide guidance during an emergency evacuation. Unfortunately, however, there may be situations where there is considerable ambiguity concerning who should be the leader. In such a case, it is quite possible that no one will take charge and try to direct the flow.

Even when someone assumes the role of leader and tries to direct the flow of pedestrian traffic, that person may be unsuccessful. In the absence of a communication system, the leader may have to rely on the spoken voice, and that may be inadequate to get the attention of most people. A good communication system may have existed prior to the emergency, but something such as an explosion or fire can knock out the system.

Even when someone assumes the role of leader and a good communication system is operative, the leader may not communicate effectively. For example, the leader may fail to provide clear, unambiguous instructions.

Even when someone assumes the role of leader, a good communication system is operative, and the leader presents clear, unambiguous instructions, the people may not heed the instructions because they are not convinced that this person is especially knowledgeable about the circumstances confronting them and about how to maximize the efficiency of the traffic flow. The leader has to be someone people recognize as being especially knowledgeable or the leader has to instill such a belief by what he/she says and how it is said.

FACTORS ONCE THE TRAFFIC FLOW IS STRONG

9. The crowd density is so great that independence of individual action is lost to a considerable extent. In a number of the case histories, it is clear from accounts by the people involved that the loss of individual action contributed substantially to the injuries and deaths occurring.

The crowd density can become so great that one cannot free oneself from the flow. Keeping one's feet can become difficult as the crush surges in some direction. People may not deliberately knock others down or trample on them; instead, the irresistible flow of the mass may cause you to bump another sharply, perhaps even knock that person to the ground. The flow of the mass may cause you to trample on someone who is down, unavoidably, despite strong efforts to avoid doing that.

In such cases, whether you are swept away from an exterior door or through it, or whether you are knocked down and trampled or you knock another down and trample that person depends on forces outside your control. It is as if you were a drop of water in a fast-flowing, turbulent stream.

10. There is a failure to keep the exterior openings clear beyond those openings. Once people are through the exterior door, their role in the situation is not ended. In order to maintain a fast flowing stream of people out of or into some structure, the area beyond the exterior door must be kept free. If people congregate immediately past the exterior opening, the escape path of those behind them becomes blocked. Furthermore, keeping the areas beyond the exterior openings free of people makes access to the structure easier for those dealing with the cause of the emergency and trying to assist injured or trapped people. Police officers, firefighters, and emergency rescue personnel will be hampered if the areas beyond the exterior openings are not clear.

We have listed those 10 factors that contributed to the catastrophes in the five cases of dysfunctional traffic flow. We will describe the condition of each factor in each of the cases of poor traffic flow (see Table 3), then we will examine the condition of each factor in the cases of good traffic flow. By contrasting the cases of poor traffic flow with the cases of good traffic flow, we hope to understand why disaster was avoided in those instances of good traffic flow.

IROQUOIS THEATRE FIRE
1. Passage Restrictions: Severe
  A. *Locked doors*: A number of the doors out of the seating areas were locked and remained so, despite the fact that an usher could have opened them. Many of the exterior doors were locked, both at the fire escapes and at the main entrances. Access to the fire escape was via two sets of doors with lock mechanisms that were hard to operate even when unlocked.
  B. *Aisles*: Although the aisles were not unduly narrow, the aisles at the rear of the seating areas, 6 feet at the narrowest, had to accommodate a particularly large crowd. The inside of the theater was oriented east and west, while the main entrance was at the south and the fire escape doors were at the north. Therefore, many people had to move to the rear and then along the back aisle in order to reach an exit door.
  C. *Dangerous steps*: Steps located immediately outside the doors to the seating areas proved hazardous as people tripped over them in the rush to flee the flames and smoke. The main staircase, especially where there was a sharp turn, was difficult for a large number of people to descend quickly without someone falling. Once someone fell, others tripped over him/her, producing a pile that blocked egress.

2. Crowd Size: 2,000
There was a large, standing-room-only crowd of about 2,000 people.

3. Path Knowledge: Moderate (?)
  A. *Familiarity*: The Iroquois was a new theater, and *Mr. Blue Beard* was the first show performed there. In all likelihood, therefore, this was the first time any of the audience had been in the building. It seems unlikely that the

audience paid special attention to the possible exit paths that could be used in an emergency. Why should they? In the upper-right-hand corner of the first page of the playbill were the words: "Absolutely Fireproof." Even people's knowledge of the path they had used when proceeding to their seats was probably shaky. In the dark, smoke-filled building, some people exiting from the rear of the gallery failed to take the necessary right turn to the stairs and proceeded straight ahead to a locked door. By the time they realized their error, fire had escaped the interior and blocked their safe return to the main stairs. Unfamiliarity with the exit path cost these people their lives.

B. *Education*: Management provided no information in the playbill or by announcement concerning possible exit pathways.

4. Emergency Planning/Training: None
Neither instruction nor training in emergency evacuation was given to theater personnel. Consequently, ushers left certain interior doors locked.

5. Perceived Outcome Severity: Extreme threat of death
The fire was extremely intense, especially in the balcony and gallery, as the draft between the open stage doors and the vents at the top and rear of the auditorium caused the flames to jet out and upward. Dense, life-threatening smoke pervaded the building. People were certainly aware that death was imminent unless they escaped.

6. Perceived Time Available: Extremely short
The fire and smoke quickly became life-threatening. Indeed, the flames burned to death some in the balcony and gallery before they could even get up out of their seats. All must have realized the extreme time pressure they were under.

7. Using Most Salient Path: Initially, other paths later
Initially, most of the audience headed for the path they had used on entering. Some tried to exit via the doors to the fire escape, which were closer to those on the north side of the seating sections. The members of the cast on stage knew about or discovered exit paths from there to the outside.

8. Leader Influence: Slight on main floor, none in balconies
Eddie Foy, from the stage, implored people to exit in a calm and orderly manner. He may have had some impact on those on the parquet, or main, floor, but at his own admission, he was unable to affect the actions of those in the balcony and gallery. Ushers exerted little, if any, crowd control.

9. Crowd Density: Extremely dense
The density, particularly on the stairs, was so great that people necessarily collided with others. If someone fell, the density forced others to step on the person or trip over him/her, even if those who followed tried their best to avoid the fallen. Furthermore, the areas where traffic merged with the traffic from above were not large enough to accommodate the sudden increase in people.

Table 3
Factors Affecting Competitive Behavior

	Iroquois Theater Fire	Cocoanut Grove Fire	Hartford Circus Fire	Beverly Hills Fire	The Who Concert Stampede	Trans World Airlines Crash	World Trade Center Bombing
1. Passage Restrictions	Severe	Severe	Severe	Severe	Severe	Adequate	Adequate
2. Crowd Size	2,000	1,000	7,500–8,000	2,500 (over 1,000 in Cabaret Room)	8,000	292	50,000
3. Path Knowledge	Moderate (?)	Limited	Moderate (?)	Very limited	Good	Good	Good
4. Emergency Planning/ Training	None	None	None	None	None	Excellent	Inadequate
5. Perceived Outcome Severity	Extreme threat of death	Extreme threat of death	Extreme threat of death	Extreme threat of death	In some areas, severe danger	Extreme threat of death	Moderate threat from smoke

6. Perceived Time Available	Extremely short	Extremely short	Extremely short	Extremely short	Extremely short	Extremely short	Long
7. Using Most Salient Path	Initially, other paths later	Initially, other paths later	Mainly paths away from the fire	Initially, later guided to other paths	Toward available entrances	Followed leaders' directions	Initially, but many waited in offices
8. Leader Influence	Slight on main floor, none in balconies	Variable, sometimes in small groups	Minimal	Mainly good	None	Excellent	When present, excellent
9. Crowd Density	Extremely dense	Extremely dense	Extremely dense	Extremely dense (especially in Cabaret Room)	Extremely dense	Dense	Dense
10. Congestion Beyond Exterior Openings	Limited problem	Severe problem	Not a problem	Severe problem initially	Severe problem	Not a problem	Not a problem

107

10. Congestion Beyond Exterior Openings: Limited problem
Initial congestion outside the front door slowed the egress, but the police were soon able to control the area, allowing easier egress and access to the building by the firefighters and the police.

COCOANUT GROVE FIRE
1. Passage Restrictions: Severe
A. *Locked doors*: A number of outside doors were locked, the most important being the emergency exit door at the top of the stairs leading out of the Melody Lounge. Management was apprehensive that open emergency doors would allow "deadbeats" to exit without paying.
B. *Inadequate exit doors*: The main entrance had one revolving door with no adjacent doors. When that door came off its frame, the people trapped inside were burned to death and further egress was impossible. Furthermore, the inner door on the exit path out of the New Lounge opened inward. The push of the crowd forced that door closed.
C. *Obstructions*: Unattached tables and chairs, especially in the Main Dining Room, were knocked over and became a hazardous obstruction.
D. *Unmarked Paths*: The hallway between the Main Dining Room and the New Lounge was unmarked and dim. Exit paths behind the bandstand were unmarked. Exterior windows were covered by interior walls, so people were not aware of them until firefighters broke through the windows and the interior walls.

2. Crowd Size: 1,000
It was Saturday night and the evening of the big Boston College–Holy Cross football game. An extremely large crowd was on hand that evening. Extra tables were set up in the Main Dining Room.

3. Path Knowledge: Limited
A. *Familiarity*: Most people knew only one way out of the building, the way they had entered. Management wanted it that way, because they feared that "deadbeats" would sneak out if they knew of alternative ways of exiting.
B. *Education*: Management deliberately did nothing to make emergency exit paths known to patrons.

4. Emergency Planning/Training: None
There was no training for personnel in emergency evacuation procedures.

5. Perceived Outcome Severity: Extreme threat of death
Once people in a given area of the club became aware of the fire, it soon became apparent that the intensity of the fire and the density of the smoke threatened imminent death.

6. Perceived Time Available: Extremely short
The fire spread very rapidly from one area of the building to another with little or no advance warning. Consequently when people started to exit, they clearly

had little time available to get out alive.

7. Using Most Salient Path: Initially, other paths later

Initially, the people in the Melody Lounge, where the fire began, headed out via the path they had entered. The emergency exit door at the top of the stairs was locked, so they proceeded to the main entrance. Most patrons in the Main Dining Room headed for the main entrance. Most patrons in the New Lounge headed for the exterior door onto Broadway. When congestion and/or fire blocked the path used on entering the club, people either discovered new pathways on their own or followed others, sometimes night club personnel, to alternative exits.

8. Leader Influence: Variable, sometimes in small groups

Some attempts at social influence failed and some succeeded. Police Captain Buccigross was seated in the New Lounge when the crowd from the Main Dining Room entered. He tried to slow their flight and got knocked down for his effort. When various night club personnel tried to aid people in finding alternative exit routes, some people followed them and some did not. For example, in the Melody Lounge, bartender John Bradley and busboy Stanley Tomaszewski led groups to safety by a back door, but many ignored their pleas for people to use that door rather than the stairway up to the first floor. Cashier Daniel Weiss, nephew of the owner, failed in his attempt to have night club personnel and patrons follow him from the basement kitchen to a distant stairway leading up to the first floor.

9. Crowd Density: Extremely dense

Throughout the club, on the stairs up from the Melody Lounge, in the lobby area before the revolving main door, in the Main Dining Room, and in the New Lounge, the crush was so severe that people lost control over their own movements. Relatives and friends often were forced apart. People were swept out through an exit door or away from one, depending on forces outside their control. People knocked into one another, even stepped on people, not through individual decisions to do so but because surges of the crowd drove them into or onto others.

10. Congestion Beyond Exterior Openings: Severe problem

The very narrow streets around the Cocoanut Grove made congestion inevitable. Approximately half the people inside the club were killed and most of the rest were burned and/or suffered from the inhalation of smoke, carbon monoxide, and acrolein. The dead and injured lay on the sidewalks and in the narrow streets. Bystanders collected quickly in this night club and hotel district, some to help, others just to observe. The police did their best to cordon off the area, thereby controlling the onlookers, providing those engaged in rescue operations with room to work, and opening paths for the ambulances.

HARTFORD CIRCUS FIRE

1. Passage Restrictions: Severe

A. *Obstructions*: The two metal animal chutes leading from the enclosed performance rings inside the tent to the cages outside obstructed passage between the north stands and the performance rings. Most of the bodies were found along the chute on the eastern side of the tent.

B. *Inadequate exit paths*: Many of the exit paths narrowed as they progressed from inside the tent toward the exit. The paths along the north and south sides of the tent were fairly narrow. They were used primarily as paths for performers, animals, and equipment rather than for egress or ingress by the public.

C. *Stands*: Loose chairs in some sections of the stands were knocked over, blocking the flow of people.

2. Crowd Size: 7,500–8,000

A large matinee crowd was present for "The Greatest Show on Earth."

3. Path Knowledge: Moderate (?)

A. *Familiarity*: The configuration of the tent was essentially the same as in prior years, so some patrons may have been familiar with the layout. However, given that the circus only performed a few shows in Hartford each summer, it seems likely that familiarity was moderate at best.

B. *Education*: The management did not alert the audience to the various possible exits either by a public announcement or by a diagram in the program. However, one could probably see the majority of the exit paths from most seats. Visual inspection, then, may have produced a moderate level of knowledge.

4. Emergency Planning/Training: None

A very meager amount of fire-fighting equipment was on hand and there was no training at all in emergency evacuation. Despite the numerous occurrences of very small fires and occasionally a larger one, the circus acted as if any fire would be a very minor one, easily extinguished by one or two people using water buckets.

5. Perceived Outcome Severity: Extreme threat of death

The fire was intense. Large flaming sheets of canvas fell on the crowd. The tent began to collapse. Severe injury or death clearly would be the fate of anyone who did not get out.

6. Perceived Time Available: Extremely short

Because the canvas was waterproofed with a paraffin and gasoline mixture, the fire spread across the canvas with great rapidity. The entire tent was consumed by fire in five to 10 minutes.

7. Using Most Salient Path: Mainly paths away from the fire

The fire started along the side wall adjacent to the main entrance, consequently most headed away from the salient main entrance, where the tent side wall was ablaze. Many headed for the large exits on either side of the bandstand at the east end of the tent. Others used the narrower exit paths along the north and south sides of the stands. Interestingly, only a relatively small number thought of crawling under the side walls of the tent.

8. Leader Influence: Minimal
The band played on. Here and there, some of the circus personnel or police assisted isolated individuals, but there was no concerted effort by anyone to direct the evacuation.

9. Crowd Density: Extremely dense
Along the animal runs especially, the density was high. People were forced into the runs, pinned against them, and sometimes caught between the bars. Density was generally high, as 7,500 to 8,000 people en masse vacated the crowded stands and then evacuated the burning tent through a limited number of exit paths, some seriously obstructed.

10. Congestion Beyond Exterior Openings: Not a problem
Pictures of the fire from outside the tent invariably show the people outside still in flight. Escapees did not stop once outside but continued to run away from the collapsing tent. Furthermore, the state police commissioner was on hand, and he took command of rescue and crowd control operations.

BEVERLY HILLS FIRE
1. Passage Restrictions: Severe
A. *Locked doors*: One, perhaps two, exit doors were locked. The locked door in the Garden Room had an open door beside it, so there was only partial restriction of flow out the rear of the Garden Room. Nevertheless, had the locked door been open, flow out of the North-South Hallway via the Garden Room would have been more rapid. As a result, more people might have escaped the Cabaret Room into the North-South Hallway and then out via the Garden Room before fire consumed the hallway. The exit door behind the drapes in the Viennese Room may have been locked, but none attempted to use that hidden door and all the people who were in the Viennese Room escaped alive.

B. *Inadequate exit doors*: The number of exterior doors was too few for the number of people inside. The lack of exit doors was an especially acute problem in the Cabaret Room.

C. *Obstructions*: Throughout the night club there were obstructions, such as unattached tables and chairs, but obstructions were especially problematic in the Cabaret Room. In the Cabaret Room, there were stairs leading to four different levels, railings between levels, and a very congested arrangement of mainly unattached tables and chairs.

D. *Unmarked paths*: The two side paths leading from the Cabaret Room to the exterior doors were circuitous and unmarked. In the darkness produced by the dense smoke and a failed electrical system, some people lost their way, then succumbed to smoke inhalation and carbon monoxide poisoning.

2.   Crowd Size: 2,500 (over 1,000 in the Cabaret Room)
Every banquet room was being used that night, and all but the Zebra Room, where the fire began, were occupied at the time of the fire. The Cabaret Room was sold out, and extra tables were set up to accommodate the large crowd.

3.   Path Knowledge: Very limited
A.   *Familiarity*: It is impossible to know how many patrons were there for the first time and just how knowledgeable repeat patrons were about the layout of the club. It seems from interviews with patrons that those on the first floor knew about the main entrance and probably about the doors at the rear leading from the Garden Room to the exterior, but nothing more. Even club personnel were unaware of some of the exits, such as the one behind the curtains in the Viennese Room. Patrons on the second floor knew of the spiral staircase but not about the service stairway to the kitchen. Furthermore, the configuration of hallways and rooms on the first floor formed a complex maze, not easily solved. People relied on guidance and information from club personnel to find their way out.
B.   *Education*: Nothing was done to educate patrons or even employees about the various exits from the building.

4.   Emergency Planning/Training: None
Although the owners had promised that such training would occur, it had not. The spread of information and the guidance of people to safety by club personnel was extemporaneous.

5.   Perceived Outcome Severity: Extreme threat of death
Although initially in many areas of the club the smoke was limited or nonexistent, the rapid spread of the fire soon made it clear that the situation was life-threatening.

6.   Perceived Time Available: Extremely short
Initially where the smoke was sparse or nonexistent, people may have felt little urgency. However, the rapid spread of the fire soon led people throughout the club to realize that immediate evacuation was necessary.

7.   Using Most Salient Path: Initially, later guided to other paths
Initially all patrons in the front on the first floor and all patrons on the second floor headed for the main entrance. People in the Garden Room or the North-South Hallway headed mainly for the rear exits off of the Garden Room. When fire cut off access to the main entrance, people relied mainly on waiters and waitresses to guide them to alternative exits.

8.   Leader Influence: Mainly good
Waiters, waitresses, busboys, and other club personnel often guided patrons they were serving to safety. People readily accepted such leadership. Busboy Walter Bailey influenced the people in the Cabaret Room to some extent—he

convinced them to begin the evacuation process—but he failed to convince them of the need to do so quickly.

9.   Crowd Density: Extremely dense (especially in the Cabaret Room)
The narrow path leading to the front entrance became packed, slowing progress there. The greatest problem with regard to density was in the Cabaret Room. When the fire entered the room, people pushed forward, forcing those in front of them to knock into others and trip over anyone who fell. As a result, a pile of people formed at one exit of the Cabaret Room, completely stopping egress there.

10. Congestion Beyond Exterior Openings: Severe problem initially
At first, people outside the various exits were slow to move away from the building, creating congestion. Consequently the egress of those inside was slowed. The police and firefighters succeeded in moving people away from the building, thereby clearing the areas around the exit doors.

THE WHO CONCERT STAMPEDE
1.   Passage Restrictions: Severe
Only a small number of entrances, all clustered together, were used. Passage through a small number of turnstiles further slowed the ingress of people.

2.   Crowd Size: 8,000
At the time of the catastrophe, there was a crowd outside of 8,000, according to a police estimate.

3.   Path Knowledge: Good
People clustered outside the entrance doors that would be used. There seemed to be little ambiguity about where they were to enter.

4.   Emergency Planning/Training: None
Neither the hired employees inside nor the meager police troop outside had any specific training in how to control the crowd on the concourse outside.

5.   Perceived Outcome Severity: In some areas, severe danger
People found the press of the crowd frightening. In an area where someone fell, that press caused a situation of severe danger. People who were down or were near the fallen realized the danger, but people on the periphery did not know that people were down and being trampled.

6.   Perceived Time Available: Extremely short
People in the vicinity of the fallen and those on the ground realized that the trampling must end quickly or serious harm would soon result.

7.   Using Most Salient Path: Toward available entrances
People in the crowd were swept along toward the entrances.

8.   Leader Influence: None
People in the crowd were unable to halt the relentless press forward. Police on the periphery did not realize that people were down and being trampled until it was too late for the 11 who died.

9.   Crowd Density: Extremely dense
The crowd was so dense that some people were lifted off the ground, sometimes losing their shoes. It became difficult, sometimes impossible, even to lift your arms over your head. Except on the periphery, there was little, if any, freedom of individual action.

10. Congestion Beyond Exterior Openings: Severe problem
The limited number of ticket takers led to a slowing of ingress. Inside the entrance doors, there was a bottleneck at the turnstiles.

TRANS WORLD AIRLINES CRASH
1.   Passage Restrictions: Adequate
The aisle and exits were adequate for rapid evacuation. Indeed, everyone got out through only three doors in two to three minutes.

2.   Crowd Size: 292
On board were 280 passengers and a crew of 12.

3.   Path Knowledge: Good
A.   Familiarity: Undoubtedly most passengers had flown before and were familiar with the general layout of a commercial plane, if not of this L1011 in particular.
B.   Education: On commercial flights, a concerted effort is made, via diagrams and preflight announcements, to alert passengers to the locations of the regular and emergency exits and to explain how to open an emergency exit. Perhaps not all passengers pay as much attention to the preflight announcements as they should, but the knowledge of passengers about exit paths was certainly good.

4.   Emergency Planning/Training: Excellent
Airlines provide flight personnel with excellent training in emergency evacuation.

5.   Perceived Outcome Severity: Extreme threat of death
Smoke and some fire were visible after the crash. Clearly the danger was extreme.

6.   Perceived Time Available: Extremely short
Given the existence of fire and the explosive nature of airplane fuel, the time available to evacuate safely was certainly short.

7.   Using Most Salient Path: Followed leaders' directions
All passengers followed the directions of the airplane personnel, using the exit the personnel designated rather than each person selecting his or her own path.

8. Leader Influence: Excellent
The crew members responsible for the passenger evacuation acted decisively, and the passengers followed directions.

9. Crowd Density: Dense
Two hundred ninety-two people exited via one aisle and three doors in two to three minutes, so the density of the flow was fairly high, but the group members maintained individual freedom of movement and did not knock one another down.

10. Congestion Beyond Exterior Openings: Not a problem
After exiting via the chutes, each person created room for the next passenger. No bottleneck occurred outside the plane.

WORLD TRADE CENTER BOMBING
1. Passage Restrictions: Adequate
The number of hallways, stairways, and exits were more or less adequate to handle exiting in most buildings, although the evacuation of tens of thousands from the Twin Towers could have been problematical if the time pressure had been great.

2. Crowd Size: 50,000
Since the explosion occurred at a time when many were out for lunch, the number of people in the World Trade Center was not as large as it might have been. About 50,000 were there when the bomb exploded.

3. Path Knowledge: Good
A. *Familiarity*: A large number of people in the buildings worked there or came there often. Some people were, of course, first time visitors, particularly in the Vista Hotel. However, questionnaire data indicated that even people who worked in one of the Twin Towers might be unfamiliar with the locations of all three stairways. Although knowledge could be considered good, it was far from perfect.
B. *Education*: Although an evacuation/training program was supposed to educate representatives of each tenant, who, in turn, were supposed to educate all members of their firm, in reality this program did a rather poor job of educating even the representatives about the possible exit paths.

4. Emergency Planning/Training: Inadequate
There was an evacuation plan, an education program for representatives from every tenant, and drills twice a year. However, the evacuation plan required the use of a communication system that was rendered inoperative in the Twin Towers, the education of representatives was inadequate, and the fire drills were a sham, since most people never left their own floors during a drill.

5. Perceived Outcome Severity: Moderate threat from smoke
The fires were confined to the areas below ground, so the major threat came from smoke. Although in some buildings the smoke became thick enough to

cause considerable discomfort, especially in Tower One, it became life threatening only for people trapped in the elevators of Tower One.

6. Perceived Time Available: Long

Because the fires occurred only below ground in the immediate area of the
blast, they were contained by the firefighters. The smoke was diluted as it
spread throughout the vast area of the Twin Towers. Consequently, people had
considerable time to evacuate or could even remain in their offices until
firefighters or police arrived.

7. Using Most Salient Path: Initially, but many waited in offices

Those who walked down in the Twin Towers used the most familiar stairs.
Indeed, many did not know the exact locations of all three stairways. A few
in Tower Two went to the roof and were evacuated by helicopter. Many waited
in their offices until firefighters or police came.

8. Leader Influence: When present, excellent

In the Vista Hotel, where the communication systems still worked, the hotel
personnel were very effective in directing people out of the building. In the
Twin Towers, the communication systems were destroyed, so people were left
on their own. Firefighters and police who made their way up the stairs undoubtedly played an important role in informing and assisting people during
the evacuation of the Twin Towers.

9. Crowd Density: Dense

Crowd density varied, but on the crucial three stairways of each of the Twin
Towers, there was considerable crowding. The density increased as you went
down due to the convergence of people from the various floors onto the stairways. Nevertheless, freedom of individual movement was still present. People
were able to allow others, such as a pregnant woman, to pass. Firefighters and
police were able to proceed upward against the flow.

10. Congestion Beyond Exterior Openings: Not a problem

Despite the large numbers of firefighters, with their equipment, the emergency
medical personnel, with their equipment, and the large number of evacuees and
bystanders, the police were able to keep the exterior openings free. Evacuees
had no trouble exiting once they reached the ground floor.

There are six commonalities among the cases of dysfunctional traffic flow. All
had severe passage restriction, large crowd size (ranging from 1,000 to 8,000), no
emergency planning/training, extremely high perceived outcome severity, extremely
short perceived time available, and high crowd density. While the existence of all
six may not be absolutely necessary for a traffic flow catastrophe, they appear to
be the most usual ingredients in situations provoking intense physical competition
among evacuees, competition resulting in injuries and jams. The four other factors,
low path knowledge, high usage of the most salient path, low leader influence, and
congestion beyond the exterior openings, played a role in some of the disasters but

not all.

The two cases of good pedestrian traffic flow had two factors in common: adequate, unblocked passageways and the lack of congestion beyond the exterior openings. Moreover, each one had other important positive features. In the TWA Crash, despite high perceived outcome severity, low perceived time available, and fairly high density, all escaped safely without severe competition for the exit space. Why? Here there was a well rehearsed plan for the leaders, effective leader influence, and, of course, an adequate passageway to safety. The TWA Crash demonstrates the value of emergency planning/training and effective leadership in dealing with an extremely dangerous emergency.

In the World Trade Center Bombing, the perceived outcome severity involved only moderate threat from smoke and the perceived time available was long. There was no overwhelming need to evacuate immediately. Furthermore, when communication existed between authority figures and the others, as in the Vista Hotel, leader influence was excellent.

THE THEORIES REVISITED

At the end of chapter 2, we posited the question: How accurate and complete is each of these theories? In light of the analysis presented in this chapter, the answer is: None are very accurate and very complete.

All three types of theories presented in the second chapter—panic theories, decision-making theories, and the distribution of urgency levels theory—suffer from a similar problem, an incompleteness of factors considered. Perhaps the most serious omission in all three types of theories is the fact that high density precludes freedom of individual action. At high density, people's movements become severely restricted. At extremely high density, people are swept along with the flow, completely unable to free themselves from the direction of that flow. Researchers in the area of crowd control are well aware of that phenomenon, but the psychological and sociological theories on emergency egress and ingress have omitted this effect of high crowd density. The omission occurs because all the theories assume that the effects of others occur through social influence processes, such as leadership or emotional contagion, not through the restriction of physical movement.

The panic theories suffer from several other problems in addition to the one of incompleteness. Social scientists, in the main, have defined "panic" as a two-component concept, with the components being high emotional arousal and irrational behavior. High emotional arousal can occur in a person and yet that person can behave logically and wisely. Likewise, a perfectly calm person can behave stupidly. Therefore, most social scientists have restricted the use of the term "panic" to instances when both high emotional arousal and irrational behavior occur. The case histories of good and poor traffic flow give little support to those theories that allot a major role to the occurrence of panic, defined in this manner. The case histories highlight two major problems with this concept of panic: (1) as usually defined, it seldom occurs; (2) even when it might have occurred, it is difficult, if not impossible, to know what was rational from the perspective of those caught in the situation.

Johnson (1988), in his analysis of the testimony of survivors of the Beverly Hills Supper Club Fire, concluded that severe pushing and shoving did not occur in the Cabaret Room until fire invaded the room. At Beverly Hills, one woman in the Main Bar froze and began screaming when the smoke became intense; but such occurrences seem to be extremely rare. The overwhelming majority of people maintain self control and evacuate in a generally civil way—until it appears that the flow is too slow for all to escape successfully. At that point, those who perceive that they are unlikely to get out alive may well use physical force in an attempt to save their own lives.

Who is to say what is rational and what is not? Knocking others aside in a head-long dash for the exit, going down a smoke-filled stairway, racing through a wall of flames, jumping from a window, or taking refuge inside one's office may in the end result in either life or death. The person deciding on a course of action is not omniscient. At the time, the person probably took the action that seemed most likely to result in safety. Afterward, with the expertise of hindsight, we can know what actions worked and what did not. If a person took a particular course of action and the result was bad, does that mean that the action was necessarily irrational, an example of panic? If a person's action ended in a result that was good, does that mean that the action was necessarily rational? Chance and circumstances beyond the knowledge of people caught in the situation can determine life or death. A major problem, then, with describing the behavior as panic is that the assumption of rationality or irrationality is usually based on the outcomes. If the outcomes were bad, the behavior is labeled as panic, but if the outcomes were good, the behavior is not labeled as panic.

Bryan (1983) in his extensive study of 335 fire incidents, mainly in homes and apartments (Project People), and in his subsequent analysis of 59 fire incidents, mainly in nursing homes, hospitals, and mental institutions (Project People II), interviewed or surveyed a large number of people who had experienced an emergency evacuation due to fire. While a number of people used the term "panic" in describing their own reactions, Bryan concluded that they were referring to their emotional feelings of anxiety and concern, not to their overt behaviors. Even in people who said that they had experienced panic, "when one examined the behavior of the participants it was determined they adopted behavioral responses that were logical, rational, functional, and usually most effective to the environmental situation of the fire incident" (Bryan, 1983, p. 141).

There is no denying that increased emotional arousal is likely during a life-threatening emergency. As Bryan's research indicates, it is these feelings of heightened arousal that most people mean when they use the term "panic." Because that is the way most people use the concept, we see some value in social scientists using the concept in the same way. However, we should not fall into the trap of assuming that whenever excessive physical competition follows high emotional feelings (panic), it is necessarily the panic that causes the competitive behaviors.

The various panic theories include some of our factors. Most of them assume that the perception or interpretation of the situation as one of extreme danger is a crucial factor in causing dysfunctional flow. In our analysis, such a perception or interpretation is reflected in the combined factors of perceived outcome severity and perceived time available. Most of the theories assume that strong leadership, especially if combined with drills, can facilitate efficient flow. In our analysis, such an assumption is reflected in the factors of leader influence and emergency planning/training. Furthermore, Smelser's Value-Added Theory of panic assumes that structural conduciveness is an important cause of dysfunctional flow. In our analysis, this assumption is reflected in the factor of passage restrictions.

Despite the fact that panic theories identify some of the important factors in dysfunctional flow, we have rejected them because they are incomplete, because it is virtually impossible to determine the rationality of actions independent of the results, and, most of all, because there is little evidence that emergencies typically induce uncontrollable emotional reactions. Panic is not the reason for dysfunctional flow.

How about the decision-making theories of Mintz and Brown? According to the decision-making analysis by Mintz, cooperation maximizes one's own gain if the others are cooperative, but competition maximizes one's own gain if the others are competitive. Therefore, it is rational that people cooperate when others cooperate but compete when others compete. In his decision-making analysis, Brown theorized that entrapment was analogous to the prisoner's dilemma, where competition maximizes one's own gain regardless of the choice of the other, but mutual cooperation maximizes one's own gain relative to mutual competition. Brown proposed that in such a situation making the competitive choice is rational. These analyses, like the panic theories, try to specify what is rational. As we have argued with regard to the panic theories, deciding upon what seemed rational from the perspective of those caught in the emergency is extremely problematic.

There are several additional problems with the decision-making analysis of Brown. One, as Brown himself acknowledged, is that people in one location of a burning building may well have a different payoff matrix than those in another location. Some of the different matrices may not be analogous to the prisoner's dilemma. Two, the outcome matrix in a case of entrapment does not have fixed outcomes. The outcome values are dynamic, changing rapidly as the threat intensifies or is brought under control. The changing matrix values may not always be analogous to the prisoner's dilemma.

We believe that it is best to avoid the unresolvable issue of what is rational and what is not. Consequently, the Distribution of Urgency Levels Theory of Kelley, Condry, Dahlke, and Hill has a lot of appeal. According to this theory any factors that increase the number of people with high urgency, such as large crowd size, the perception of high outcome severity, and the perception of low time available, will cause an increase in jams and a slowing of the flow, while any factors that reduce the number with high urgency, such as calm leadership acts, will cause a decrease in jams and facilitate the flow. There is nothing in the theory concerning what is rational or irrational.

The theory, however, has two major weaknesses. One, like all the existing theories, it is incomplete. Some important factors, such as the role of crowd density in restricting freedom of movement, are omitted. Two, the theoreticians regarded a situation where most or all have low urgency as one resulting in efficient flow. Except for an occasional false start—"After you." "No, after you."—pedestrian movement should be excellent. Our examination of case histories, however, reveals that a situation where everyone is low in urgency—but a real threat is on the way—is a situation likely to end in poor flow. For example, in the Cabaret Room at Beverly Hills, the initial warning by a busboy caused few to experience feelings of high urgency. The exiting, consequently, was slow, slower than could have been achieved. As a result, when the fire suddenly entered the Cabaret Room, there was too little time left for all to exit safely. People pushed aggressively, and a jam resulted.

In conclusion, none of the existing theoretical analyses is very complete and accurate. We have identified the 10 factors that should be included in a complete analysis of emergency egress or ingress. These factors, in combination, determine the behaviors of the people involved. We turn next to an analysis of how they combine with each other.

1. REACTIONS TO THE INITIAL WARNING

The initial warning that an emergency exists and movement is necessary can be communicated from others, such as verbally or by an alarm, or by physical evidence, such as seeing or smelling smoke.

A. If the initial warning does not indicate clearly that the outcome severity is high and the time available is low (Factors 5 and 6), people are likely to move slowly, perhaps not at all, until they become convinced that the emergency is genuine.

B. If the initial warning does indicate clearly that the outcome severity is high and the time available is low (Factors 5 and 6), people do experience increased arousal (they may have subjective feelings of panic), but they move in a fairly orderly flow that is sustained at a relatively high rate of speed.

2. INITIAL DIRECTION OF MOVEMENT

A. Initially people usually move along the most salient path (Factor 7).

B. If people have knowledge of an alternative path (Factor 3), are trained to use an alternative path (Factor 4), or are directed toward another path by some leader (Factor 8), and movement along the alternative path seems more likely to result in faster or safer escape, people are likely to use an alternative path.

3. SLOWING OF THE FLOW

A. Passage restrictions (Factor 1), large crowd size (Factor 2), lack of knowledge of alternative paths (Factor 3), lack of emergency planning/training (Factor 4), use of the most salient path (Factor 7), lack of good leader influence (Factor 8), and congestion beyond the exterior openings (Factor 10) combine to produce slow, congested movement by a large number of people along the same or a very small number of paths.

B. If, given a person's perceptions of the outcome severity and the time available (Factors 5 and 6), it seems to the person that the flow is fast enough for he or she to escape successfully, the person will not try to disrupt the flow.

C. If a person comes to believe that severe injury or death is likely if he or she maintains the present position in the flow, the person will either leave the flow and search for another path or force his or her way forward at the expense of others. The choice between searching for another path and aggressing along the present path will be made on the basis of which seems more likely to result in successful escape.

4. HIGH CROWD DENSITY

A. When density (Factor 9) becomes so severe that freedom of individual movement is severely curtailed, the decision making of individuals is largely irrelevant.

B. The direction of further movement then results mainly from the overall movement of the crowd as a whole.

Chapter 11

Prescriptions for Success

How can the occurrence of egress and ingress disasters be avoided or at least minimized? Our analysis provides some answers to that question.

We have titled this chapter "Prescriptions for Success," because the prescription is different, depending on one's role in the situation. We have divided the roles into four categories: (1) owner/management; (2) government; (3) personnel; and (4) patrons.

OWNER/MANAGEMENT

After the Cocoanut Grove Fire, the National Fire Protection Association (NFPA) prepared a report on the catastrophe. The report contained a section entitled "How It Could Have Been Prevented." This one-page section identified the changes necessary to transform the building "from a death trap into a place of assembly reasonably safe for public occupancy" (Moulton, 1943, p. 11). According to the report "no structural changes are involved and . . . nothing suggested would call for any large expenditure" (Moulton, 1943, p. 11). Add some exit and exit path signs. Alter some doors to swing outward or with the exit flow, not swing inward or against the flow. Keep all exit doors unlocked. Construct a direct door from the Melody Lounge to the kitchen. Replace the revolving front door with doors that swing outward. Remove or replace all highly combustible decorations. Add several fire doors to the first floor. Remove a few obstructions, such as a partition at the exit of the New Cocktail Lounge. Widen one exit door. Enclose the stairs to the second floor. Install automatic sprinklers throughout the basement. (The heat-sensitive automatic sprinkler is an old invention that was available before the beginning of the twentieth century.)

There would have been some cost involved in making these changes, not trivial, but not exorbitant either. Some "deadbeats" might have departed surreptitiously without paying, but a few strategically placed employees would have been able to minimize that risk.

Why did owner Barnie Welansky continue to operate what the NFPA report afterward labeled a "death trap"? One possibility is that Barnie Welansky did not care enough about the lives of the employees and patrons of the Cocoanut Grove to spend the money it would have taken to transform an unsafe building into a safe one. However, that is an implausible explanation. Barnie Welansky cared about his brother, who was there and nominally in charge that night, since Barnie was in the hospital. Barnie Welansky cared about his nephew Daniel Weiss, who worked weekends as a cashier and who was working in the Melody Lounge that night. He had contributed generously to pay for Daniel's education. Some of the employees and patrons were longtime acquaintances of Welansky. Barnie Welansky himself would have been there had it not been for his recent heart attack. It is hard to believe that Barnie Welansky was indifferent to whether his brother, his nephew, his friends, his acquaintances, and he himself lived or died.

It is unlikely that the owners and managers at any of the sites of the five disasters were so callous as to deliberately put so many lives, sometimes including the lives of family members and themselves, at risk in order to save a relatively small, though not inconsequential, amount of money. There is a more plausible explanation. They believed that they could save money (by not implementing unnecessary expenditures) without putting themselves, loved ones, workers, and customers at risk.

How risky was it to leave certain doors locked at the Cocoanut Grove? How risky was it to have flammable material hanging from the ceiling in the Melody Lounge? How risky was it to have a revolving door as the only door at the main entrance? What was the risk of almost 500 people dying in a fire at the Cocoanut Grove on the night of November 28, 1942?

Psychological research on how people assess risk provides a likely answer for why Barnie Welansky allowed the Cocoanut Grove to be a death trap: He did not believe that it was one! A number of psychological processes lead people such as Barnie Welansky to assess risk inaccurately (Plous, 1993).

1. If an event is extremely negative, we tend to deny that the event will occur. We use the psychological mechanism of denial to avoid coming to grips with the possibility that a horrible event could happen to us.

2. People rate themselves as more likely than others to experience positive events and less likely than others to experience negative events. Hence, owners and managers are likely to believe that a fire or a bombing is less likely to happen in their place than in the places of others.

3. People tend to overestimate the probability of conjunctive events. A combination of events is called conjunctive if the combination is stated in the form "both A and B." For example, what is the probability that a particular building will be free from fire both today and tomorrow if the probability that it is safe from fire is 99 percent each day? Even though the odds in favor of safety are extremely high on any given day, when you start to calculate the odds in favor of safety over a long time span, the risk becomes considerable. People do not fully appreciate the long-term risk. Evidently people get so anchored, or focused, on the single event probability that they have great difficulty determining the probability of the compound

events. In reality, a building that has a 99 percent chance of being free from fire on any single day has a less than 1 percent chance of being free from fire over a 500-day period. The problem is analogous to the problem confronting the automobile driver or passenger who must decide whether or not to buckle the seat belt. The probability of being in an accident on any given occasion is extremely small, but the probability of being in an accident sometime during one's life is higher than most people realize.

4. People resist changing a prior probability estimate when confronted with new information. Once an owner or a manager judges a building to be safe, that person is unlikely to alter the judgment much even if an inspector were to present new evidence that the building was unsafe.

5. Supporters of a given position feel safer after relatively minor, noncatastrophic accidents, although opponents feel less safe. An interesting thing about the catastrophes we have described is that in some cases they were preceded by events of a similar kind, though considerably less catastrophic ones. Beverly Hills was virtually destroyed by fire in 1970, but that fire occurred at night so no one was hurt. The same owners, Dick Schilling and his three sons, still operated the club on the horrible night of May 28, 1977. Before The Who Concert Stampede at Riverfront Coliseum in Cincinnati, there had been severe crowd management problems at almost every major rock concert, though nobody had died as a result. At the time of the Hartford Circus Fire, the Ringling Brothers & Barnum and Bailey Circus had experienced a number of fires in its recent past. In Cleveland in 1942, a fire in the menagerie tent burned many animals to death, although no humans were killed. According to testimony by circus employees, there may have been as many as a dozen previous fires in 1944, including one on the side wall canvas in Providence, Rhode Island, on July 4, just two days before the Hartford fire. All of the prior fires that year were quickly extinguished with a few pails of water. The research evidence indicates that people who believe a structure is safe would view such prior fires, because they had not led to loss of human life, as proving the adequacy of safeguards, and they would actually feel safer than they had originally. People who doubted the safety of the structure would view such events with alarm and feel less safe than they had before, but an owner or manager is not likely to be that kind of person.

6. People tend to be overconfident that their judgments and decisions are correct. Consequently, owners or mangers are likely to be overconfident about their decisions and fail to take certain safeguards, such as adding an extra exit door or implementing a rigorous training program in emergency evacuation for employees. The official risk estimate by NASA for its 25th mission, the fatal *Challenger* disaster, was one major failure in 100,000 launches. This estimate is approximately equal to an assessment that if you launched a shuttle every day, you would have only one catastrophic failure in three centuries of launches. Vitali Skylarov, minister of Power and Electrification in the Ukraine, was quoted as saying two months before the nuclear accident at Chernobyl: "The odds of a meltdown are one in 10,000 years" (Plous, 1993, p. 217).

These six somewhat interrelated psychological processes, (1) the denial of the occurrence of extremely negative events, (2) the belief that negative events are more likely to happen to others rather than self, (3) the overestimation of the probability of conjunctive events, (4) the resistance to changing a prior risk assessment, (5) the belief that one is actually safer than one originally thought following a noncata-strophic accident, and (6) overconfidence in one's judgments and decisions, combine to lead owners and managers to genuinely believe that the conditions at their structure are safe.

Psychological research on judgment and decision making identifies certain techniques that are sometimes effective in counteracting those six processes (Plous, 1993): (1) have the owner/manager imagine vividly what a catastrophic event, such as a fire, would be like; (2) have the owner/manager think about and list the various ways in which the negative event could occur; (3) have the owner/manager keep accurate records of how often similar events have occurred in the past; (4) persuade the owner/manager to get a risk assessment from a knowledgeable, but independent, third party; (5) when estimating the probability of conjunctive events from the probability of independent single events, have the owner/manager first give an estimate of the probability of a single event and then have him or her multiply the probabilities together to get the probability of the conjunctive events; (6) convince the owner that feelings of confidence need to be recalibrated downward due to the existence of overconfidence; and (7) have the owner/manager list possible reasons why his or her judgment or decision may be wrong.

Do not be overconfident about being able to change the view of an owner or manager. A formidable set of psychological processes are arrayed against change. Consequently, government officials may have to compel an owner or manager to take the proper safeguards.

If an owner or manager were interested in safeguarding the structure and the people who use it, our list of 10 factors related to the occurrence of good or poor traffic flow provides a useful framework:

1. Passage Restrictions: Make sure that pathways and exits are adequate for the maximum number of people using them. These pathways and exits should be well lighted, clearly marked, and free from obstruction.

2. Crowd Size: Keep the number of people down to a number the structure can accommodate comfortably.

3. Path Knowledge: Provide workers and patrons with information about emergency exit paths, for instance, use diagrams in programs or public announce-ments before performances begin.

4. Emergency Planning/Training: Develop a good emergency plan, one with contingency plans for various possibilities, and provide adequate training in the implementation of the plan.

5. Perceived Outcome Severity, and 6. Perceived Time Available: In constructing or remodeling the structure, include safeguards such as fire alarms and sprinklers, so that people are unlikely to be caught in a situation where serious injury or death will result if they do not escape in a very short time.

7. Using Most Salient Path: Counteract the tendency of people to use the most salient path by including in the emergency plan specifications about the use of different paths by different groups. Furthermore, as stated before, make the patrons aware of alternative paths and encourage them to use the closest path in an emergency.

8. Leader Influence: Maximize the effectiveness of leader influence by training workers so that they know and can execute leadership acts automatically. If possible, provide a good communication system by which the leaders can communicate easily with patrons and with each other.

9. Crowd Density: The layout of the structure and the emergency plan, in combination, should direct people in a way that avoids large masses moving along the same path or through bottlenecks. The number of patrons should be limited to the maximum allowed by building and safety codes.

10. Congestion Beyond Exterior Openings: The emergency plan should specify who is responsible for crowd control beyond the exterior openings and how that control is to be achieved.

GOVERNMENT

Owners and managers cannot be relied upon to provide a completely safe structure. Government must enact laws that mandate a safe structure and these laws must be rigidly enforced.

Although the laws specifying the number and size of exits, the width of hallways and stairways, and the like have been based in the past on untested assumptions about how fast a group of people actually moves, there is a growing body of empirical data on the actual flow rates of crowds (Nelson & MacLennan, 1995; Pauls, 1995). Increasingly, therefore, building codes and safety codes are based on solid assumptions about the flow rates of pedestrians. However, stringent laws will do no good unless they are rigidly enforced. On the cover sheet of the NFPA Cocoanut Grove Report are listed the "Fundamentals of Fire Safety": "1. Honest, non-political enforcement of building codes and fire laws. 2. Competent, technically trained enforcement personnel. 3. Educated public opinion. Without these fundamentals, laws and codes are wholly ineffective" (Moulton, 1943, p. 1).

It is certainly possible that some building inspectors approve unsatisfactory structures because they have been bribed or because they are repaying a political favor. Outright corruption is not the only problem. Sometimes the inspectors know little about architecture or construction and do not understand fully the laws they are to enforce. Sometimes inspectors themselves view the regulations as too picky and require compliance only on some subset of the entire set of requirements. Usually inspections are conducted in daytime when the structure is empty, so the existence of certain bottlenecks may be overlooked. Sometimes it is unclear which governmental unit is responsible for conducting inspections or for examining building plans. Is the state, county, or city government responsible for these things? Within a given level of government, which office is responsible for enforcing the laws? If a violation is found, does the government insist on the problem being corrected? Sometimes inspectors note a violation and receive a verbal commitment from the owner to take appropriate action, but there is no follow-up to see that the changes necessary for compliance have been made. Or, if there is follow-up and the required changes have not been made, the government may be slow to close the building or bring legal action against the owner. Frequently the inspecting and enforcing agencies lack enough personnel to inspect adequately buildings of public assembly on a regular basis and to prosecute vigorously building code violators. To avoid the type of catastrophes described in this book, there must be stringent laws, strictly enforced by a sufficient number of honest, knowledgeable government officials.

Beverly Hills is a case in point. The Southgate building inspector was not particularly knowledgeable about construction or architecture. The city of Southgate had one part-time inspector, and the state of Kentucky had too few inspectors to inspect rigorously and often all buildings of public assembly. Responsibility for approving remodeling plans and for conducting inspections was ambiguous. It was not completely clear what responsibilities Kentucky had and what responsibilities Southgate had. All inspections were done in the day, none at night when the difficulties of exiting the Cabaret Room would have been apparent. Although inspectors made certain demands and received promises that certain corrective actions would be taken, there was seldom any follow-up to see that those corrections had been made. For instance, the promised training program for Beverly Hills personnel never occurred. Sometimes, the owners of Beverly Hills proceeded with new construction before a permit was obtained, but the inspectors never ordered a halt to the construction and never prosecuted the owners for the violation.

As a consequence of the tragedy at Beverly Hills, the state of Kentucky made major changes. A new building code was adopted. A new department, Housing, Building, and Construction, was created to regulate the construction and use of buildings. A licensed architect was chosen to head the department, and he was given assurances that he and his department would be free from political influence. A professional engineer was hired as the new fire marshal. A staff of attorneys was assigned to the department, so that quick legal action could be taken when needed. An education program for inspectors was implemented. Inspectors were ordered to demand strict compliance with all laws and to use the new legal staff, if necessary, to enforce compliance. The number of field inspectors was increased from 65 to almost 100.

Gradually public demand for vigorous enforcement waned. By the end of 1982, the total staff of the new agency had been reduced to 121 from its high-water mark of almost 160, and the number of field inspectors had decreased from almost 100 to 74.

PERSONNEL

If management unilaterally acts to make the structure as safe as possible or if management is forced to do so by the government, personnel will be working under optimal conditions. Personnel will be made familiar with all exit paths, and they will be well trained in an effective emergency plan. However, management and government may not have produced ideal conditions. Emergency training may be lacking. If so, what should a worker do?

There are a number of steps a worker should take. (1) When you have free time, perhaps before or after your working hours, explore the building until you are totally familiar with all parts, especially all exterior doors. Ideally you should become so familiar with all avenues of escape that you could find your way in the dark. Smoke can totally obscure your vision. Smoke irritates the eyes, causing them to shut involuntarily. (2) If an emergency occurs, impart any information you have about the emergency to others, especially if you are certain about the accuracy of your information. (3) Do not minimize the danger when conveying information to others (Proulx & Sime, 1991). When people are warned initially about severe danger, they generally advance in an orderly manner. When the danger is minimized, they generally advance quite slowly, so slowly that when danger does arrive, there is not enough time for all the remaining people to escape alive. (4) When instructing others about how to proceed, be as clear as possible. Mention prominent landmarks they can locate as they go. Repeat your instructions in order to enhance people's memory of your instructions. (5) As soon as possible, sound the fire alarm if there is one and call the fire department. (6) Assume responsibility for the safety of any patrons or visitors in your area. Guide them to safety immediately after sounding the alarm. You know the way; they do not. If time permits, guide people in other areas of the structure to safety as well.

PATRONS

As a patron you have no control over the structure itself or the behaviors of the personnel. However there are important things you can do. (1) Given a choice, you should patronize those establishments that provide a safe environment. For example, select a hotel that has sprinklers over one that does not. (2) If management provides you with information about exit routes, learn that information. Pay attention to announcements or written information about emergency procedures and exit paths and learn the material. (3) On your own initiative, learn the layout of the structure. If you are entering a restaurant, a night club, a theater, an airplane, or whatever, try to learn the physical layout and the locations of the various possible exits. A little extra attention as you enter may save your life. (4) If there is an emergency, call the fire department as soon as possible and sound the fire alarm if there is one. (5) At the slightest indication of possible danger, get out. Research indicates that people are slow to react to the appearance of smoke or to the sound of a fire alarm (Tong & Canter, 1985). Even when people recognize the sound as a fire alarm, they may assume—when there is no visible sign of a fire—that the equipment is being tested, it is malfunctioning, or the alarm just signals the occurrence of a fire drill. Don't hesitate. Exit immediately. Delay could be fatal. (6) If there is a fire, follow fire safety precautions such as not opening a hot door, closing doors behind you, staying down below the level of the smoke, and not using elevators. (7) Don't panic. Try to control your arousal level. Very high arousal causes the narrowing of attention, the failure to consider a wide range of options, and the performance of dominant responses. Stay calm and consider possibilities that did not come to mind immediately. If you are in a circus tent, how about crawling under the side wall rather than trying to get out through one of the regular exits?

CONCLUSIONS

We have identified the 10 factors that cause dysfunctional pedestrian traffic flow during an emergency. In this chapter, we have provided prescriptions for eliminating those factors or for adapting to them if they are present. Adapting to them, of course, is less desirable than eliminating them. For anyone caught in an emergency situation such as those we have described, all you can do is to function in a way that maximizes the odds that you and others around you will get out alive. Often good luck is more important than good decision making.

In researching the case histories reported in this book, we were impressed with how level headed and heroic the vast majority of people were during emergency egress or ingress. Often people risked their own lives in an attempt to save others. Severe physical competition for exit space only occurred once it became likely that everyone was not going to escape alive.

The conditions that produce dysfunctional traffic flow are not a thing of the past. In December of 1986, 97 people died at a fire in the DuPont Plaza Hotel in San Juan, Puerto Rico. The casino, where most of the deaths occurred, had an inadequate number of exits, only two, and one of the exit doors opened inward. In December of 1995, a fire at a year-end school party in Dabwali, India, killed about 365. About 1,000 students and relatives were packed into a community hall and an attached tent. The hall had only two entrances, the main entrance and a side entrance, which was locked. People were trampled in their egress through the one open door. Eventually the locked door was forced open. The tent had linen bunting, which caught fire and fell on the people inside. In March of 1996, about 150 people were killed in a fire at the Ozone Disco Pub in Quezon City, Philippines. The discothèque, in a suburb of Manila, was overcrowded with students celebrating the end of the school year. A narrow corridor separated the dance floor from the single entrance. People were trampled to death along that narrow corridor. As the French saying indicates: The more things change, the more they are the same thing.

Josephine Nicolosi almost lost her life in the Triangle Shirtwaist Factory Fire on March 25, 1911. The fire, on the eighth, ninth, and 10th floors of the Asch Building in New York City killed 146 employees of the Triangle Shirtwaist Company. If we had included a sixth case history of poor pedestrian traffic flow, most likely it would have been the Triangle Fire. After escaping, Nicolosi helplessly watched the bodies of her dead fellow workers being lowered by ropes. Many years later, on March 19, 1958, she witnessed a fire at a firm where women's undergarments were made. The company was on the fourth floor of a building near her apartment. As she again watched bodies being lowered in baskets by rope, she cried out: "What good have been all the years? The fire still burns" (Stein, 1962, p. 214).

People seem not to learn from past examples. Oh, there is typically a strong initial reaction, so that governmental reforms usually follow a major catastrophe. Over the years, people become lax once more, as can be seen in the aftermath of the Beverly Hills Fire. Hopefully, this book will lead people to remain vigilant. If owners/managers and government officials act as we have prescribed, emergencies with poor pedestrian traffic flow will be less frequent. If personnel and patrons act as we have prescribed, efficient egress or ingress during emergencies will be more frequent.

References

Benzaquin, P. (1959). *Holocaust!* New York: Henry Holt.

Best, R. L. (1977). *Reconstruction of a tragedy: The Beverly Hills Supper Club fire.* Quincy, MA: National Fire Protection Association.

Brown, R. (1965). *Social psychology.* New York: Free Press.

Bryan, J. L. (1983). Implications for codes and behavior models from the analysis of behavior response patterns in fire situations as selected from the Project People and Project People II study programs (NBS-GCR-83-425). Washington, DC: US Department of Commerce, National Bureau of Standards, Center for Fire Research and U.S. Department of Health and Human Services.

Chertkoff, J. M., Kushigian, R. H., & McCool, M. A., Jr. (1996). Interdependent exiting: The effects of group size, time limit, and gender on the coordination of exiting. *Journal of Environmental Psychology, 16,* 109–121.

Cohn, H. S., & Bollier, D. (1991). *The great Hartford circus fire: Creative settlement of mass disasters.* New Haven: Yale University Press.

Delaney, J., & Greenfield, J. (1979, December 5). Coliseum capacity figure too high, officials say. *The Cincinnati Enquirer,* p. B-1.

Dunn, C. F. (1979). *Report of the special prosecutor: The Beverly Hills Supper Club fire, Southgate, Kentucky, May 28, 1977.* Commonwealth of Kentucky.

Fahy, R. J., & Proulx, G. (1995). Collective common sense: A study of human behavior during the World Trade Center evacuation. *NFPA Journal, 89,* 59–67.

Foy, E., & Harlow, A. F. (1928). *Clowning through life.* New York: E. P. Dutton.

Freud, S. (1922). *Group psychology and the analysis of the ego.* London: Hogarth.

Gold, M. (1948). *The Front Street Theatre (from its beginning to 1838).* Unpublished master's thesis, Johns Hopkins University, Baltimore, MD.

Guenzel, L. (1993). *Retrospects: The Iroquois Theatre fire.* Elmhurst, IL: Theatre Historical Society of America.

Hickey, E. J. (1945). *Report of commissioner of State Police as state fire marshal to state's attorney for Hartford County concerning the fire in Hartford on July*

6, 1944, at the Ringling Bros.-Barnum & Bailey Combined Shows, Inc. Connecticut.

Investigative report to the governor: Beverly Hills Supper Club fire: May 28, 1977 (1977). Commonwealth of Kentucky.

Isner, M. S., & Klem, T. J. (1993). *Fire investigation report: World Trade Center explosion and fire, New York, New York, February 26, 1993.* Quincy, MA: National Fire Protection Association.

Janis, J. L., & Mann, L. (1977). *Decision making: A psychological analysis of conflict, choice, and commitment.* New York: Free Press.

Johnson, N. R. (1987). Panic at "The Who concert stampede." An empirical assessment. *Social Problems, 34,* 362–373.

———. (1988). Fire in a crowded theater: A descriptive investigation of the emergence of panic. *International Journal of Mass Emergencies and Disasters, 6,* 7–26.

Johnston, D. M., & Johnson, N. R. (1988). Role extension in disaster: Employee behavior at the Beverly Hills Supper Club fire. *Sociological Focus, 22,* 39–51.

Kelley, H. H., Condry, J. C., Jr., Dahlke, A. E., & Hill, A. H. (1965). Collective behavior in a simulated panic situation. *Journal of Experimental Social Psychology, 1,* 20–54.

Keyes, E. (1984). *Cocoanut Grove.* New York: Atheneum.

Kimball, W. Y. (1944). Hartford Circus holocaust. *Quarterly of the National Fire Protection Association, 38,* 9–20.

Kirson, A. (1993). *Terror in the Towers: Amazing stories from the World Trade Center disaster.* New York: Random House.

Kleinfield, N. R. (1993, February 27). First darkness, then came the smoke. *The New York Times,* pp. 1, 22.

La Piere, R. (1938). *Collective behavior.* New York: McGraw-Hill.

Lawson, R. G. (1984). *Beverly Hills: The anatomy of a nightclub fire.* Athens, OH: Ohio University Press.

Le Bon, G. (1960). *The crowd.* New York: Viking. (Originally published 1895).

Luce, R. D., & Raiffa, H. (1957). *Games and decisions.* New York: Wiley.

Mathews, T., Breslau, K., Rogers, P., & Peyser, M. (1993, March 8). A shaken city's towering inferno. *Newsweek,* pp. 26–27.

McDougall, W. (1920). *The group mind.* Cambridge, UK: Cambridge University Press.

McFadden, R. D. (1992, July 31). 292 escape burning jetliner at Kennedy Airport. *The New York Times,* pp. A1, B2.

———. (1993, February 27). Blast hits Trade Center, bomb suspected; 5 killed, thousands flee smoke in Towers. *The New York Times,* pp. 1, 22.

Mintz, A. (1951). Non-adaptive group behavior. *Journal of Abnormal and Social Psychology, 46,* 150–159.

Moulton, R. S. (1943). *The Cocoanut Grove Night Club fire: Boston, November 28, 1942.* Boston, MA: National Fire Protection Association.

Murphy, J. E. (1944, July 7). Fire spread fast, eyewitness says. *The New York*

Times, p. 11.

Myers, S. L. (1992, July 31). Passengers recount scene of fearful calm in flaming plane's cabin. *The New York Times*, p. B2.

National Transportation Safety Board (1993). *Aircraft accident report: Aborted takeoff shortly after liftoff, Trans World Airlines flight 843, Lockheed L-1011, N11002, John F. Kennedy International Airport, Jamaica, New York, July 30, 1992 (NTSB/AAR-93/04, PB93-910404)*. Washington, DC: Author.

Nelson, H. E. B., & MacLennan, H. A. (1995). Emergency movement. In P. J. DiNenno, C. L. Beyler, R.L.P. Custer, W. D. Walton, J. M. Watts, Jr., D. Drysdale, & J. R. Hall, Jr. (Eds.), *SFPE handbook of fire protection engineering*. (2nd ed., pp. 3-286–3-295). Quincy and Boston, MA: National Fire Protection Association & Society of Fire Protection Engineers.

Out went the gas. (1895, December 28). *The Baltimore Sun*, p. 8.

Pauls, J. (1995). Movement of people. In P. J. DiNenno, C. L. Beyler, R.L.P. Custer, W. D. Walton, J. M. Watts, Jr., D. Drysdale, & J. R. Hall, Jr. (Eds.), *SFPE handbook of fire protection engineering*. (2nd ed., pp. 3-263–3-285). Quincy and Boston, MA: National Fire Protection Association & Society of Fire Protection Engineers.

Plous, S. (1993). *The psychology of judgment and decision making*. New York: McGraw-Hill.

Proulx, G., & Sime, J. D. (1991). To prevent "panic" in an underground emergency: Why not tell people the truth? In G. Cox & B. Langford (Eds.), *Fire safety science—Proceedings of the third international symposium* (pp. 843–852). London and New York: Elsevier Applied Science.

Sarah Seigle's death. (1895, December 28). *The Baltimore Sun*, p. 8.

Schultz, D. P. (1964). *Panic behavior: Discussion and readings*. New York: Random House.

'76 study recommended Coliseum reduce "festival seating." (1979, December 5). *The Cincinnati Enquirer*, p. A-1.

Sime, J. D. (1985). Movement toward the familiar: Person and place affiliation in a fire entrapment setting. *Environment and Behavior, 17*, 697–724.

Smelser, N. J. (1963). *Theory of collective behavior*. New York: Free Press.

Stein, L. (1962). *The Triangle fire*. Philadelphia: J. B. Lippincott.

Theatre employees. (1895, December 28). *The Baltimore Sun*, p. 8.

Those leaking pipes. (1895, December 30). *The Baltimore Sun*, p. 10.

Told by young girls. (1895, December 28). *The Baltimore Sun*, p. 8.

Tong, D., & Canter, D. (1985). Informative warnings: In situ evaluations of fire alarms. *Fire Safety Journal, 9*, 265–279.

Treaster, J. B. (1992, July 31). Swift escape proves value of long-practiced procedures. *The New York Times*, p. B2.

Various experiences. (1895, December 28). *The Baltimore Sun*, p. 8.

Went back for his wife. (1895, December 28). *The Baltimore Sun*, p. 8.

White, E. J. (1992). *Famous American diasters* (chapter 5, pp. 110–139). Boston: Creative Television Associates.

Zajonc, R. B. (1965). Social facilitation. *Science, 149*, 269–274.

Annotated Bibliography

This section is intended as a guide for those who would like to read further about the events described in the book. Included are our major sources of information, not all of them.

CHAPTER 1: INTRODUCTION

1. *The Baltimore Sun*. Detailed accounts of the Front Street Theatre Fire, including many feature articles, can be found in *The Baltimore Sun* of Saturday, December 28, 1895, and Monday, December 30, 1895. Short articles can be found in some subsequent editions, leading up to the report on the grand jury investigations, which appeared in the Saturday *Baltimore Sun* of January 11, 1896.

2. Gold, M. (1948). *The Front Street Theatre (from its beginning to 1838)*. Unpublished master's thesis, Johns Hopkins University, Baltimore, MD. The fire of 1895 is mentioned only briefly on pages 13–14, but the thesis does contain a picture of the exterior of the theatre as it appeared in 1829 and presumably as it still appeared in 1895. This picture is taken from a woodcarving in the archives of the Peale Museum, Baltimore, Maryland.

3. *The New York Times*. A full column on the front page of Saturday, December 28, 1895, was devoted to the event.

CHAPTER 3: IROQUOIS THEATRE FIRE, DECEMBER 30, 1903

1. *The Chicago Tribune*. *The Chicago Tribune* had extensive coverage of the fire in its edition of Thursday, December 31, 1903. Numerous follow-up articles appeared throughout the month of January 1904, culminating in the grand jury report on Tuesday, January 26, 1904.

2. Foy, E., & Harlow, A. F. (1928). *Clowning through life*. New York: E. P. Dutton. In Foy's autobiography, all of chapter 20 is devoted to the Iroquois Theatre Fire. The chapter contains a picture of Eddie Foy in his costume as Sister Anne in *Mr. Blue Beard*.

3. Guenzel, L. (1993). *Retrospects: The Iroquois Theatre fire*. Elmhurst, IL:

Theatre Historical Society of America. This is perhaps the most valuable single source on the Iroquois Theatre Fire. It comes close to being the kind of investigative report done in more recent years by the National Fire Protection Association.

Louis Guenzel was born in Prussia in 1860 and came to the United States in 1892. He was working as an architect in Chicago at the time of the Iroquois Fire. On the very day of the fire, the German consul Dr. Wever, an acquaintance of Guenzel, requested that Guenzel, on behalf of the government of Prussia, examine the building and submit a report of his findings concerning the cause of the disaster. Guenzel agreed, and with a pass provided by the city government, first entered the Iroquois Theatre at 10:00 A.M. on December 31, 1903, the morning after the fire. He spent several weeks investigating the structure, making precise measurements, drawing plans, and taking photographs. His detailed account of the condition of the building, the exit paths, the exits, and the progress of the fire is invaluable. Some of the detailed plans of the building are reproduced in our book.

4. *The New York Times.* On Thursday, December 31, 1903, *The New York Times* devoted all of the first two pages and a third of page 3 to the Iroquois Theatre Fire.

CHAPTER 4: COCOANUT GROVE NIGHT CLUB FIRE, NOVEMBER 28, 1942

1. Benzaquin, P. (1959). *Holocaust!* New York: Henry Holt.
2. Keyes, E. (1984). *Cocoanut Grove.* New York: Atheneum. *Holocaust* and *Cocoanut Grove* are two very interesting and comprehensive books dealing with the Cocoanut Grove Fire and its aftermath. They are about equal in thoroughness of coverage and quality of writing. The Benzaquin book has an index, but the Keyes book does not. Although the Keyes book is 25 years newer, it contains no new revelations.
3. *The Boston Globe, The Boston Herald, The Boston Advertiser, The Boston Traveler,* and *The Boston Daily Record.* For a solid week, from November 29, 1942 to December 5, 1942, all five Boston papers contained extensive coverage of the Cocoanut Grove disaster. Following the stories over that week highlights the fact that early accounts were incomplete and contained errors and misconceptions. Gradually, a somewhat more accurate account emerged, but without the later books and investigative reports, it would be hard to obtain a clear, accurate view of what happened.
4. Moulton, R. S. (1943). *The Cocoanut Grove Night Club fire: Boston, November 28, 1942.* Boston: National Fire Protection Association. This informative investigative report covers a description and plan of the property, the story of the progress of the fire, the implementation of the fire-fighting, rescue, and emergency treatment operations, the plausability of various theories of the cause, the behaviors of occupants, and recommendations for improving fire safety.
5. White, E. J. (1992). *Famous American disasters* (chapter 5, pp. 110–139). Boston: Creative Television Associates. This is a concise but adequate descrip-

tion of the fire. It contains a large number of excellent photographs.

CHAPTER 5: HARTFORD CIRCUS FIRE, JULY 6, 1944

1. Cohn, H. S., & Bollier, D. (1991). *The great Hartford circus fire: Creative settlement of mass disasters*. New Haven: Yale University Press. Chapter 1, "Fire at the Circus," covers the fire itself, and chapter 6, "Fire Safety Reforms," covers the disclosures of certain investigative reports. The rest of the book deals with legal issues and controversies arising out of the fire.
2. *The Hartford Courant* and *The Hartford Times*. There was extensive coverage of the fire, with front page headlines, on Friday, July 7, 1944, and Saturday, July 8, 1944. The fire and its aftermath continued to receive front page coverage in both papers for many days, but it was competing for space with news from World War II.
3. Hickey, E. J. (1945). *Report of commissioner of State Police as state fire marshal to state's attorney for Hartford County concerning the fire in Hartford on July 6, 1944, at the Ringling Bros.-Barnum & Bailey Combined Shows, Inc.* Connecticut. This is the report of the commissioner of state police, based on the testimony from a large number of witnesses, including circus management, performers, and personnel, Hartford police, and Hartford firefighters. It is a concise statement of what happened. The report covers the lack of proper inspection, the lack of preparedness, the problems with exit pathways, and the paraffin-gasoline mixture used to coat the canvas.
4. Kimball, W. Y. (1944). Hartford Circus holocaust. *Quarterly of the National Fire Protection Association, 38*, 9–20. This is a clear, concise description of the fire, including a description of the tent and a discussion of the exits, the progress of the fire, and the waterproofing mixture.
5. *The New York Times*. On July 7, 1944, a column on the first page and all of p. 11 was devoted to the Hartford Circus Fire. The fire was front page news again on July 8, 1944.

CHAPTER 6: BEVERLY HILLS SUPPER CLUB FIRE, MAY 28, 1977

1. Best, R. L. (1977). *Reconstruction of a tragedy: The Beverly Hills Supper Club fire*. Quincy, MA: National Fire Protection Association. This is an extensive report, including an examination of the history of the structure, the structure at the time of the fire, the behaviors of firefighters, police, emergency personnel, and the occupants, including information obtained from interviews and question-naires. There are excellent floor plans and pictures. It probably contains a few errors, but it is a very impressive and detailed report.
2. *The Cincinnati Enquirer* and *The Louisville Courier-Journal*. These newspapers gave the story virtually the entire front page on May 30, 1977, and a number of additional inside pages. The story continued to be big news for days afterward. Both papers did retrospective articles on the fire on the 20th anniversary, with *The Cincinnati Enquirer* including a special 12-page section on the fire, "The Fire that still rages," in the edition of Sunday, May 25, 1997.
3. Dunn, C. F. (1979). *Report of the special prosecutor: The Beverly Hills Supper Club fire, Southgate, Kentucky, May 28, 1977*. Commonwealth of Kentucky.

This report focuses primarily on the legal culpability of people involved with the fire, but it does a clear job of presenting the facts of the disaster, attempting to resolve several points of disagreement in past reports, how the two women who died on the second floor came to be there, and whether there was a significant delay in calling the fire department. The final recommendation against prosecuting anyone involved, based on legal arguments, is clearly reasoned.

4. *Investigative report to the governor: Beverly Hills Supper Club fire: May 28, 1977* (1977). Commonwealth of Kentucky. This report was highly critical of the management of Beverly Hills with regard to code violations in construction and with regard to alleged delays in calling the fire department and in notifying occupants of the fire.

5. Johnson, N. R. (1988). Fire in a crowded theater: A descriptive investigation of the emergence of panic. *International Journal of Mass Emergencies and Disasters, 6,* 7–26. This article contains an interesting analysis of the transcripts from police interviews of occupants after the fire.

6. Lawson, R. G. (1984). *Beverly Hills: The anatomy of a nightclub fire.* Athens, OH: Ohio University Press. This book was written by a lawyer who was on the staff of Cecil Dunn, the special prosecutor who investigated the fire. It is the most complete and probably the most accurate account of what happened at Beverly Hills. It is a gripping book, and is well written.

CHAPTER 7: THE WHO CONCERT STAMPEDE, DECEMBER 3, 1979

1. *The Cincinnati Enquirer.* The entire front page of the December 4, 1979, and the December 5, 1979, *Cincinnati Enquirer* contained coverage of The Who concert disaster, and there was additional coverage on interior pages. On December 5, 1979, there was a special report section on the tragedy.

2. *Time* and *Newsweek.* Each, in their issues of December 7, 1979, devoted over a page to the tragedy.

3. Johnson, N. R. (1987). Panic at "The Who concert stampede": An empirical assessment. *Social Problems, 34,* 362–373. This article contains an extremely clear description of the sequence of events. An informative analysis is done, based on the interview responses of patrons and police.

CHAPTER 8: TRANS WORLD AIRLINES JET CRASH, JULY 30, 1992

1. National Transportation Safety Board (1993). *Aircraft accident report: Aborted takeoff shortly after liftoff, Trans World Airlines flight 843, Lockheed L-1011, N11002, John F. Kennedy International Airport, Jamaica, New York, July 30, 1992 (NTSB/AAR-93/04, PB93-910404).* Washington, DC: Author. This is a very clear, very complete presentation of the relevant factual information and conclusions concerning the aborted takeoff and evacuation of TWA 843.

2. *The New York Times.* The crash of TWA flight 843 was a major story on July 31, and August 1, 1992, receiving front page coverage and virtually a full page in the Metro section each day. *The New York Times* account of why the crash occurred is totally different from the truth, as revealed in the NTSB report.

CHAPTER 9: WORLD TRADE CENTER BOMBING, FEBRUARY 26, 1993

1. Isner, M. S., & Klem, T. J. (1993). *Fire investigation report: World Trade Center explosion and fire, New York, New York, February 26, 1993.* Quincy, MA: National Fire Protection Association. This is a clear, well written report describing the explosion, its effects, and the human responses to it, including the evacuation process.
2. Kirson, A. (1993). *Terror in the Towers: Amazing stories from the World Trade Center disaster.* New York: Random House. Although written essentially as a book for junior-high or senior-high level readers, this book is interesting, informative reading for people of any age. The book, complete with an index, gives an engrossing account of many aspects of the behaviors of the occupants and the people who tried to help them.
3. *Newsweek* and *Time.* Both magazines on March 8, 1993, had extensive coverage of the bombing.
4. *The New York Times.* The World Trade Center bombing dominated the front page on February 27, 1993, and was the subject of numerous feature articles in the Metro section. It continued to be an important story for days afterward.

Index

About the Authors

JEROME M. CHERTKOFF is Professor of Psychology at Indiana University.

RUSSELL H. KUSHIGIAN, Ph.D. Indiana University, is a consultant specializing in emergency preparedness.

ISBN 0-275-96268-7

90000>

EAN

9 780275 962685

HARDCOVER BAR CODE